HOW TO BEAT UNEMPLOYMENT

HOW TO BEAT UNEMPLOYMENT

RICHARD LAYARD

with assistance from
ANDREW SENTANCE

OXFORD UNIVERSITY PRESS

1986

Oxford University Press, Walton Street, Oxford OX2 6DP

Oxford New York Toronto
Delhi Bombay Calcutta Madras Karachi
Petaling Jaya Singapore Hong Kong Tokyo
Nairobi Dar es Salaam Cape Town
Melbourne Auckland

and associated companies in
Beirut Berlin Ibadan Nicosia

Oxford is a trade mark of Oxford University Press

Published in the United States by
Oxford University Press, New York

British Library Cataloguing in Publication Data
Layard, Richard
How to beat unemployment.
1. Unemployment—Great Britain 2. Manpower
policy—Great Britain. 3. Great Britain
—Full employment policies
I. Title II. Sentance, Andrew
331.13°77°0941   HD5765.A6
ISBN 0–19–877265–3
ISBN 0–19–877264–5 Pbk

Library of Congress Cataloging in Publication Data
Layard, P. R. G. (P. Richard G.)
How to beat unemployment.
Bibliography: p.
Includes index.
1. Unemployment. 2. Unemployment—Effect of
inflation. 3. Full employment policies. 4. Unemploy-
ment—Great Britain. I. Title.
HD5707.5.L39 1986   331.13°77°0941   86–12684
ISBN 0–19–877265–3
ISBN 0–19–877264–5 (pbk.)

Set by Katerprint Typesetting Services, Oxford
Printed in Great Britain by
Richard Clay (The Chaucer Press) Ltd
Bungay, Suffolk

To
Rudi Dornbusch
Liberator of minds

Contents

Contents

Acknowledgements

Most of the ideas in this book come from working with other people. First there are my colleagues in the Centre for Labour Economics at the London School of Economics. We have been trying together to make sense of these problems for years, and my special debts are to Richard Jackman and Stephen Nickell. There is no adequate way I can thank them. The empirical analysis in Part I draws very heavily on work with Nickell, and the policy analysis in Part II draws equally heavily on work with Jackman, and with George Johnson (of the University of Michigan). I have also been generously educated by Orley Ashenfelter (of Princeton University), Charlie Bean, Willem Buiter, David Grubb, Chris Pissarides, and Sushil Wadhwani.

The other strong influence comes from friends at the Massachusetts Institute of Technology, where they do the best macro-economics in the world. Through our joint work for the Centre for European Policy Studies, Rudi Dornbusch and Olivier Blanchard have taught me so much about those issues.

The book was read by Olivier Blanchard, Gavyn Davies, Richard Jackman, Anita Jackson, Clive Smee, and David Stanton. Their comments were excellent, but they are not responsible for the result.

Andrew Sentance is. He provided massive and invaluable help on all aspects of the work and it would never have been done without him. The book was splendidly typed by Ellen Byrne and Phyllis Gamble.

Richard Layard

March 1986

1

The Argument

Unemployment in Britain is now as high as in the early 1930s. It is the major social problem of our time. But many people doubt whether it can be reduced. As in the 1930s, they consider it an act of God—the product of forces beyond our power to control. Yet after the 1930s came the 1950s and 1960s, when unemployment was lower than in any previous period (see Fig. 1). So clearly the fact that unemployment has risen does not of itself mean that it cannot come down.

At first sight the natural way to deal with unemployment is simply to increase spending. Either the government can spend more itself, or it can let private citizens spend more by taxing them less. Either method will encourage spending, and thus create jobs for those producing the extra output. This is the long-standing 'Keynesian' answer to unemployment. And it is at least half true.

THE PROBLEM

But there is an obvious problem. How can we ensure that the spending does not lead to more inflation? At first unemployment certainly falls. But how can we be sure that after a while inflation does not start creeping up? For when unemployment falls, employers will find it more difficult to fill their vacancies. So they will try to attract workers by paying more than the going rate. At the same time unions will feel in a stronger position to push for wage increases. So wage inflation could be a very real problem, leading eventually to higher prices in the shops.

There is also another potential source of inflation. If we try to expand the economy, fears of inflation could undermine confidence in our currency. This could lead to a fall in the value of the pound, so that we would have to pay more in pounds for

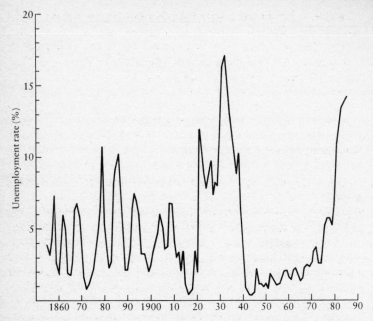

Fig. 1 Unemployment in the United Kingdom, 1855–1985.

anything we imported. Thus prices in general would tend to rise and the original fears be confirmed.

SHOULD WE ADJUST TO UNEMPLOYMENT?

So is there nothing we can do? It is easy to say that the problems are too big, and that the best thing is to adjust to unemployment. On this line of thinking, our only mistake lies in failing to educate for leisure.

This view is absolutely wrong and immoral. We now have over 3 million unemployed, of whom $1\frac{1}{4}$ million have been out of work for over a year. Most of them do not want leisure. They are depressed. Only a job can make them feel needed and socially useful. Besides, so long as they are out of work, our national output is far below what it could be, making most of us poorer.

Thus the urgent need is to reduce unemployment. But we must also contain inflation. If we think hard, we *can* find a realistic strategy for achieving both these objectives. In this chapter, I shall outline such a strategy in fairly dogmatic terms, and in the rest of the book explain it at more leisure.

THE STRATEGY

The strategy is based on four rules.

Rule 1: Create jobs for those kinds of workers who are unemployed.
Do not spend money across the board, so that employers are trying to take on as many more programmers as machinists. For it is machinists who are unemployed, not programmers. If firms try to hire more programmers, they will bid up their wages. But if they go for less skilled people, there will be much less upwards pressure on wages, since there are so many people of that kind who are unemployed.

Applying this rule means that, when the government spends money, it should spend it on activities employing lots of low-skilled people or on people who are currently unemployed. The work must also be socially useful. One obvious area is construction. Much of the fabric of our schools, hospitals, sewers, and roads is crumbling, and expenditure on this 'infrastructure' is biased towards less-skilled people. We need to spend more.

In particular we need to have programmes which mainly employ unemployed people. The government should guarantee a one-year placement on such a programme to everybody who has been out of work for more than a year. This would do more than any other single policy to reduce the horrendous total of unemployment.

Equally, when the government cuts taxes or gives subsidies, these should be directed at the kinds of workers who are unemployed. Thus, employers should be given a large subsidy if they employ people who have been out of work for over a year. There should also be a general cut in employers' National Insurance

contributions for low-paid workers—which could be financed in
part by higher taxes on skilled workers. And National Insurance
contributions should be eliminated altogether on new jobs
created in high unemployment areas.

These steps would all increase the demand for less-skilled
workers. But unemployment is the difference between supply
and demand. So rule 2 aims to reduce the supply of the less-
skilled.

Rule 2: Train, train and retrain the less-skilled.
We must reduce the number of untrained people by shifting
them up the skill ladder. This will reduce the shortages of labour
that already exist higher up.

But, however careful we are, the danger of wage inflation will
always be there. We want to reduce unemployment to well
below 2 million, and this cannot be done unless we have an
incomes policy.

Rule 3: We must have an incomes policy.
In the late 1970s we only had $1\frac{1}{4}$ million unemployed. But then
we also had an incomes policy. The policy had its ups and
downs, or to be precise its downs and ups. Between October
1975 and October 1977 wage inflation fell from 29 per cent to 8
per cent. The policy was then somewhat relaxed and wage
inflation rose to 12 per cent in the year to April 1978, and 13 per
cent in the year to April 1979.[1] The policy was then abandoned
altogether. But it had in fact brought inflation to much lower
than before the incomes policy began. In retrospect it is clear
that we could not possibly have had the almost-tolerable level of
unemployment of $1\frac{1}{4}$ million at that time, had we not had the
incomes policy. It is essential that once again we allow ourselves
this weapon against inflation, and do not use unemployment as
the only bludgeon.

But we do not have to have the same kind of incomes policy.
Centralized incomes policies of the kind used in the 1970s
override free collective bargaining and inherently cannot survive
long. A better approach would be to use financial sanctions, and
to permit free collective bargaining. There would be a norm for

the growth in hourly earnings that an employer was allowed to pay, and he would pay a stiff tax if he went over the norm.

Additional ways of reducing unemployment would involve directly attacking the rigidities in the labour market which, as we shall see, have contributed to the rise of unemployment. These rigidities include employment protection, social security upon request, and trade union power. But policies on these matters will take time, and in the meantime the need for action is urgent.

With the aid of our first three rules we should be able to contain wage inflation. But there is also the problem of import prices, which together with wages and productivity determine the prices of things in the shops. The main influence which Britain has over its import prices comes from its influence over the exchange rate. This leads to rule 4.

Rule 4: Defend the pound, where necessary, by higher interest rates.
If the government spends more and cuts taxes, there is always the danger that this will cause a run on the pound, forcing down its value. This would mean that the pound buys fewer dollars. So more pounds would be needed to buy a Cadillac—or a Volkswagen. The result would be higher prices in the shops.

The government has two ways to defend the pound. It can buy pounds in exchange for foreign currency. This reduces our foreign exchange reserves, and its effects cannot always be relied on. A more reliable approach is to raise interest rates. This makes foreigners more willing to lend money to Britain. For this purpose they have to buy pounds. So the flight from the pound is reversed, and its value recovers. Experience has shown over and over again that this method works. Provided we are willing to use it (and known to be willing), there is no reason why the value of the pound should cause us problems. To put the matter another way, since higher interest rates go with less money, we must be willing to contain the growth of our money supply when this is needed to protect the exchange rate.

When Mitterand tried expanding the French economy in 1982 he did not follow this rule, and he also scared the financial

markets with big wage increases and a programme of nationali-
zation. We can succeed where he initially failed.

If we expanded the economy and prevented a fall in the
exchange rate, real interest rates would need to be somewhat
higher than they would otherwise be. But the difference would
not be great. For these days British real interest rates are basically determined by world real interest rates. We can, however,
vary our rates a little as a matter of policy, and this will be
sufficient to defend the exchange rate.

Some people think that high interest rates mean the end of life.
But in fact an economy can survive high real interest rates,
provided there is enough demand for output coming from the
government budget. This is exactly what has happened in the
US. And budget expansion there did not lead to a fall in the value
of the currency. Nor need it here.

COUNTER-ARGUMENTS

In the second part of the book we shall go into the detail of
policy design a lot more carefully. But at this stage it is worth
looking at some common objections to any attempt to deal with
unemployment. Fortunately these are mostly myths. Four myths
are particularly common.

*Myth 1: Extra money spending will only raise prices and not
output.*
This is a most misleading argument. We have already seen how
we could expand output without increasing inflation. We also
have the example of the USA to look at. They have not deflated
their economy; instead they have used the budget to expand
spending. This has brought unemployment down to much the
same level as in 1979. By contrast Britain has moved since 1979
to much less expansionary budgets, and unemployment has
trebled. Much the same has happened in Germany as here. If we
now had less deflation, we could greatly reduce unemployment.

The argument to the contrary is often phrased as follows.
'Over the last 20 years spending in money terms has risen by 12
per cent per annum, prices by 10 per cent, and output by only 2

per cent. Hence, a negligible fraction of any higher money spending will go into output rather than prices. There cannot be any lack of demand.'

The conclusion is false. It is true that in the long run the growth of potential output depends only on real forces in the economy and not on the level of money spending. But a *change* in the growth rate of money spending can have profound effects on the level of output relative to potential. For example, between 1980 and 1984 the growth rate of money spending in Britain fell from 17 per cent a year to 6 per cent. This was associated with a massive contraction in output relative to potential. The US recession in 1982 was also accompanied by a fall in the growth of money spending. But the next year the Americans had the sense to reverse this fall. If we did the same, we too could have a big fall in unemployment. The reason money spending matters is that inflation has its own inertia, so that cuts in the growth of money spending cut output, and boosts to it increase output. So policies to increase money spending *would* reduce unemployment.

But if we increased public spending and cut taxes, this would increase the government's budget deficit and thus increase its borrowing. This leads us to the next myth.

Myth 2: We cannot have higher spending and lower taxes because the burden of public debt would become intolerable.
This is a common belief. If one talks to voters about unemployment policy, they ask (reasonably enough) how it will be financed. If you say 'By borrowing more', the typical voter is likely to say 'You can forget it'. So deeply has the propaganda about good housekeeping gone into the British soul that some people have even forgotten that they borrowed to buy their own house. It is therefore essential to establish the difference between responsible and irresponsible expansion.

Our policies *would* widen the gap between public expenditure and tax receipts. This gap (or deficit) can only be covered by borrowing more, which increases the stock of public debt. Is the public debt now so large that we cannot contemplate such a move?

To examine this question we have to look at the debt relative to the national income from which interest on the debt has to be paid. If we do this, we find that our national debt is now lower (relative to national income) than in most of the last two centuries. It has fallen sharply since the Second World War, as Figure 2 shows. On present government plans it is set to fall for the rest of the decade.

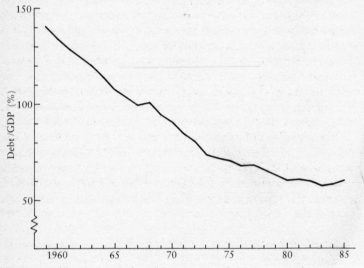

Fig. 2   Public Sector Debt as Percentage of GDP (at market prices), 1959–85

So some reflation would be possible with no increase in the ratio of debt to income. But is this the most that we should contemplate? Not necessarily. All schools of economics, from the University of Chicago leftwards, agree that in a recession it is appropriate for the debt/income ratio to rise. For a recession causes a fall in tax receipts and a rise in outlays on unemployment benefits. Both of these changes increase the deficit. There is nothing wrong with this increase, provided that the ratio of debt to income eventually stabilizes once better times have arrived. If we pursue sensible policies now, we can expect that better times will come and then the crutch of deficit spending will be less necessary. Investment will move to a permanently higher level, and this will be greatly helped if world real interest rates fall, as they must eventually. Once investment is back up, there will then be no need for further increases in the ratio of public debt to national income.

Another point should also be remembered. There is no reason why the government should not borrow money for projects which automatically pay for themselves in money coming back to the Exchequer. This applies to most of what is normally called public investment as well as to much of education, health, and road-building, which increase the country's tax base. Debt corresponding to genuine government investments should be excluded from our calculations of the debt. Viewed in this light, the government must currently be running a substantial surplus on current account, and a rise in its total debt is quite acceptable.

But will financial markets see it that way? Or will they insist on higher real interest rates as the price for holding a larger volume of debt? The first point is that our real interest rates are basically determined by the general level of rates prevailing in the rest of the world. However, the relation between our rates and foreign rates may be partly affected by the volume of our debt relative to the debts of foreign governments. But then comes the obvious point that at present the debts of foreign governments (especially the US government) are growing very much faster than ours. Even if we had a more expansionary policy, we should not reverse this situation. So there is no reason why our real interest rates should increase much if the policies in this book were pursued. Rates might occasionally need to rise to defend the value of the pound, but this would be less necessary if the arguments behind the policies were better understood.

So much for our remedies. The next myth, which is very common, relates to the causes of unemployment.

Myth 3: Unemployment has risen because modern technology replaces people by machines. It will never come down.
If this were so, the situation would be pretty hopeless. But the analysis is wrong. Technology has been replacing people by

machines since the beginning of time, yet unemployment has not been steadily rising. In fact there is no clear trend in unemployment, as Figure 1 shows. The great productivity breakthroughs of the past did not lead to prolonged general unemployment. We had the typewriter, the telephone, the electric motor, the internal combustion engine, the jet engine, and the plastics revolution. Particular workers often lost their jobs. But there was no general tendency to rising unemployment.

Where technical change actually happens, there are of course changes in employment. Sometimes it goes up (as in the high-tech industries), sometimes it goes down (as with the containerization in the docks). Either way there is dislocation while new patterns of employment are established. But one would expect, if anything, that there would be more dislocation in periods when productivity growth was unusually rapid. Yet productivity growth today is *not* unusually rapid. It was, by historical standards, high in the 1950s and 1960s, but unemployment then was unusually low. In the 1970s productivity growth fell, yet unemployment increased.

In the 1980s, productivity growth rose again, but is no higher than in the full-employment 1950s and 1960s. And the major country with the fastest productivity growth has the lowest unemployment—Japan. So let us bury for ever the idea that productivity growth as such is the problem.

Of course, if output does not grow when productivity does, there *is* a real problem. For productivity is measured by output per worker. So if output does not rise and output per worker does, fewer workers are needed. Output today is low relative to productivity. But that is a problem of low output rather than high productivity.

Why is output low? Some people say it is because of satiation—people now have all they need. That view is an insult to those who live in shabby houses with ill-fed children. There may be some Hampstead trendies or busy stockbrokers for whom extra cash would do no good, but to talk of satiation in general is immoral. The fact is that output is low not because people do not want more, but because they do not have the money to spend. Thus a major aim of this book is to explain the amount of spending that goes on. This brings us to the last myth.

Myth 4: Things are going well again and the time for any action is past.
This is absolute nonsense. Things are going very badly. Though output has been rising for five years, it is still not very much higher than in 1979.

People in work have of course done reasonably well, and profits are now booming. But economic policy is about the use of resources, and our resources are grossly underutilized. Our labour resources are as underutilized as they were in the early 1930s. This is as much of a disgrace now as it was then. Moreover in the 1930s unemployment fell steadily from 1933 onwards, whereas on present policies any major fall is unlikely now. Any argument that expansionary measures have failed in the past is irrelevant today, when we have so much more slack.

Only six years ago we had under 6 per cent unemployment, now 13 per cent. So it is quite unacceptable to say that many of the unemployed are now unemployable—except in so far as they have been made so by the policies that have been pursued.

Whether the policies were right or not up to now, they are now clearly not working. *Low inflation is not bringing a return to full employment*, as the government claimed it would. For inflation is not a cause of unemployment. Inflation is bad for other reasons, and if governments try to reduce it without using incomes policy, this causes unemployment. Priorities must now shift from cutting inflation to cutting unemployment (while controlling inflation). A total rethink of policy is required.

That is why this book has been written. I have given a rather dogmatic summary here of its main arguments. But the time has come to proceed more calmly, step by step, beginning with the causes of unemployment before coming to the cures.

THE BOOK

Let me explain the layout of the book. Part I explains why unemployment has risen. It focuses on the critical issue of the relation between unemployment and inflation. It shows that many 'supply-side' factors have worsened this relationship, but that in addition cuts in the 'demand' for output have led to massive job loss.

Part II offers a way out that would enable us to cut unemployment to the levels of the late 1970s, without increasing inflation. The 'demand' for output has to be increased, but in a way that enables us to 'supply' the output without extra inflation.

Thus the layout of Part II mirrors that of Part I, with the supply side and the demand side being viewed in tandem. There is also in Part I a chapter rejecting the view that unemployment is caused by technology, and a corresponding chapter in Part II rejecting work-sharing and early retirement as a cure. Each chapter ends with a summary.

President Truman once asked for a one-armed economist because he was fed up with being told 'on the one hand, on the other'. But on unemployment issues there is, in fact, wide agreement among British economists, and I believe the majority would share the general line of argument in this book.

PART 1

WHY HAS UNEMPLOYMENT RISEN?

2

The Basic Facts About Unemployment

TRENDS

Unemployment in Britain has risen in most years since 1966 and only fallen sharply in two (1973 and 1979). But most of the growth has occurred between 1974 and 1976 and between 1980 and 1982—after the first and second oil price rises respectively. This is shown in Figure 3.

Unemployment has now reached a level equal to the average of 1930–4.[1] But, even more depressing, it has now been rising continuously for six years, whereas in the 1930s it was already falling sharply by the fourth year of the depression.

Figure 3 also shows recent unemployment experience in Europe. This has been in many ways similar to Britain, but the average level of unemployment has not gone so high.

The US experience is in sharp contrast: though unemployment has trended upwards somewhat since the 1960s boom (associated with the Vietnam War), it is now little higher than in the 1950s. Moreover it fell sharply between 1982 to 1984, due to expansionary government budgets. The US experience should be constantly in the minds of those who believe that our recent rises in unemployment are permanent, or induced by high technology.

DEFINITION

The numbers in Figure 3 are based on standardized international definitions. People are counted as unemployed if they are seeking work but do not have it.

Thus to be unemployed, a person has to be out of work *and* looking for work. The first part of the concept is very clear—we can all see whether somebody is not at work. The second concept is somewhat more fuzzy, since there are many levels of intensity with which people may seek work. The concept is

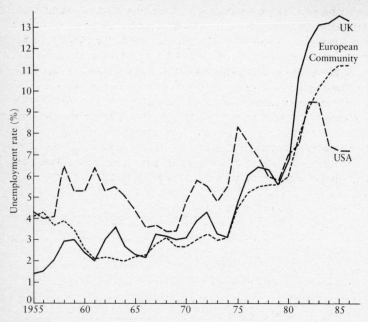

Fig. 3. Standardized Unemployment Rates for UK, USA and European Community.

Note: European Community refers to France, Germany, Italy, UK and the Benelux countries.

especially unclear in relation to those married women who have not been working but now start keeping their eyes open for a suitable opening. Thus, male unemployment is easier to think about than female unemployment. This is especially so for males aged 25–55, for nearly all of these who are not employed are unemployed (apart from 3 per cent, most of whom are invalids or students).

It is therefore interesting to look separately at male unemployment (see Table 1). In terms of this, Britain compares much less favourably with other countries than in terms of overall unemployment (which was shown in Fig. 3). This is because our official registered unemployment figures are not based on numbers seeking work but on the numbers of job-seekers receiving Unemployment Benefit or Supplementary Benefit (or National Insurance credits). Married women are not normally eligible for Supplementary Benefit, nor for Unemployment Benefit if they opted out of making National Insurance contributions. Thus official female unemployment in Britain is very much lower than male unemployment. When the standardized figures shown in Figure 3 are produced by the OECD, they attempt to adjust for this, but they are only partly successful. So figures of male unemployment may be the best guides we have to the comparative unemployment situation in different countries. They certainly highlight the appalling situation in Britain.

Table 1. Male Unemployment Rates, 1984

	Per cent
UK	13.1
France	7.7
Germany	7.6
Italy	6.6
Sweden	3.0
US	7.2

By this stage you may be wondering whether the concept of unemployment means anything at all. I would say emphatically, it does. First, it reflects wasted resources. If 10 per cent less of the work-force is employed, output will be lower by around 10 per cent (depending on how long the situation persists and who are unemployed). Second, unemployment reflects human suffering—in terms of low income and low self-esteem.

Consider, first, income. In the 1930s the income levels on the dole were much lower than today both in real terms and relative to income in work.[2] So the suffering was greater. As between countries, the incomes of the unemployed (relative to the employed) are lower in the US than in Britain, and lower in Britain than in Europe.[3]

As regards self-esteem, the effect of unemployment depends a lot on how long a person has been unemployed. There is much evidence that people's morale sinks progressively as their unemployment lengthens. So it is very important to know how long people have been unemployed.

HOW LONG DOES IT LAST?

The answer in Britain is 'Depressingly long'. In fact, nearly half of all unemployed men have now been unemployed for over a year, and the 'average' unemployed man has been unemployed for a year and a quarter.

Even more striking, most of the increase in unemployment has been in long-term unemployment. This is shown in Figure 4. The number of long-term unemployed men (out for over a year) has risen since 1974 from around 100,000 to over a million.

There is an important corollary to this. The number of people who become unemployed each year has risen relatively little.

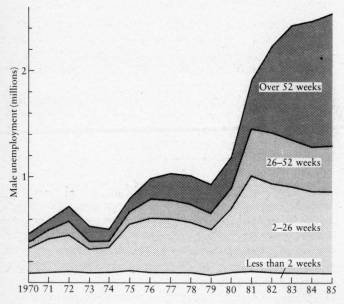

Fig. 4. Male Unemployment by Duration, 1970–85.

This can be seen by looking in Figure 4 at the number of newly unemployed people with less than two weeks' unemployment experience. It has risen relatively little. For example it was the same in 1975 as in 1985, though total unemployment was up by a factor of nearly three.

If there has been little increase in the number of people who become unemployed, this means that most of the suffering implied in extra unemployment has been piled onto a relatively small number of people. The majority of people now, as earlier, are never unemployed, while those who *are* unemployed nowadays really get it in the neck.

In this context it is useful to remember a simple rule of thumb. This says that, when unemployment is constant, the number of people who are unemployed at any time equals the number who become unemployed each week *times* the average number of weeks they remain unemployed.

Unemployment = Entrants per week × Weeks unemployed.

By analogy, the number of students *equals* the number of first-year students *times* the length of course. In the school of unemployment the number of students has risen mainly not because of new entrants but because of a depressing increase in the length of the course.

Our formula makes it clear that 13 per cent unemployment could reflect two extreme cases (or anything in between):

A. Everyone becomes unemployed once a year, for on average 13 per cent of the year, or

B. 13 per cent become unemployed each year, for on average a year. It happens that B is almost exactly the case.

As we shall see later on, this very fact provides an important clue about how to reduce unemployment: we should concentrate on reducing long-term unemployment, and avoid reducing the proportion of people who become unemployed. For this latter proportion is a powerful force restraining wage inflation, while long-term unemployment is a total waste.

In fact it is reasonable to ask why, when unemployment has risen, most of the increase has been concentrated on long-term unemployment. Might this even give us some idea as to why unemployment has stayed high in the first place? Some suggestive evidence comes from comparing the durations of unemployment in different countries and relating this to their social security systems. As Figure 5 shows, unemployment is very much shorter in Sweden and the US than in the main European countries. Why is this? An obvious factor is the social security system. In the US, Unemployment Insurance runs out after six months. After that the unemployed can in some states get a much reduced income on 'social assistance', but in many states (including 'enlightened' Massachusetts) a childless man who has been out of work for over six months gets nothing. In Sweden benefit lasts a maximum of 300 days.[4] By then the person will normally have been offered a place on a training or work programme—and if he refuses that, he ceases to be eligible for benefit. By contrast, in Germany benefits continue indefinitely (though at a reduced rate after a year). The same is true in France. In Britain for somebody already on Supplementary Benefit there is no reduction in income whatever as time goes on.

It is noticeable that the countries which have open-ended social security not only have high long-term unemployment but have also experienced the largest rises in unemployment. This raises the question as to whether, when countries are subjected to a shock (such as the second oil price rise) they are more likely to develop a culture of unemployment if they have open-ended benefits. If so, the benefit system may make it more difficult to reduce unemployment in Europe, unless specific measures are developed relating to the long-term unemployed.

HOW PEOPLE BECOME UNEMPLOYED

In this discussion I have scrupulously avoided the use of the term 'voluntary unemployment', as it is a fundamentally unhelpful concept. Unemployment is, of course, affected by individual choices but by much else besides (see Ch. 4). However, it is reasonable to ask how individuals actually come to be unemployed. The majority of unemployed men have either lost their job through redundancy or have never had a job. The proportion

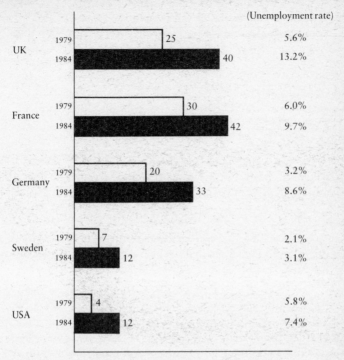

Fig. 5. Percentage of Unemployed Adults out of Work for Over a Year.

who had been dismissed was 44 per cent in 1979, rising to 60 per cent in 1981 and falling again to 44 per cent in 1984. In addition, the proportion of unemployed men who had never worked before was around 10 per cent in each year. Among women the proportion who were dismissed is smaller, and many of them are married women trying to get back to work after child-rearing.[5] The detailed picture is in Table 2.

OCCUPATION AND AGE

After this overall view, it is time to ask who the unemployed actually are. What are their skills? How old are they? Where do

Table 2. How People Came to be Unemployed, 1981

	Men	Married women	Single women
Following dismissal from regular job	60	29	27
Following resignation from regular job	16	29	20
After leaving casual job	4	7	5
After voluntary interruption of work	6	31	11
Seeking first regular job	14	4	37
	100	100	100

they live and what industries do they come from? The answer is that they are typically low-skilled, young, from the North of England, and with a background in manufacturing or construction.

Let us start with the skill mix. In Britain in 1983, 84 per cent of unemployed men were manual workers, half of them semi- or unskilled. The corresponding unemployment rates were:[6]

Non-manual	5 per cent
Skilled manual	12 per cent
Semi- and unskilled	23 per cent

There is nothing new about these differentials, which incidentally reflect differences in the number of people becoming unemployed rather than how long they have been unemployed. In fact, the differentials are as old as time. Ten or fifteen years ago, as now, semi- and unskilled workers were roughly four times as likely to be unemployed as non-manual workers.[7]

Unemployment rates are now much higher for young people than for older people (see Table 3). Their higher unemployment rate arises entirely because they are more likely to become unemployed; but once unemployed, they remain so for a shorter period than older people.

High youth unemployment is due partly to the general economic situation and partly to the level of youth wages. Since the labour market went sour in the 1970s, job prospects have probably declined more for young people than for others, as firms have cut back on hiring. But since 1979 everyone leaving school

Table 3. Male Unemployment Rates by Age, January (per cent)

	Under 18	18–19	20–24	25–54	55–59	Total
1976	12.3	11.2	10.0	4.8	4.7	6.9
1980	10.3	10.7	9.3	5.5	5.7	7.0
1985	22.3	29.2	22.5	13.7	18.7	16.6

aged 16 has been guaranteed a one-year place on what is now the Youth Training Scheme. As a result unemployment rates have risen no faster for the young than for the middle-aged. One would of course have hoped that the Youth Training Scheme would have all but eliminated youth unemployment. Instead the unemployment rate of under 18s (which does not include those on the scheme) has remained obstinately high, presumably reflecting individual choice.

As regards pay, in Germany, where youth pay is relatively lower than in Britain, the youth unemployment rate is about the same as the adult unemployment rate.[8] But in Britain, there is evidence that between 1965 and 1975 increases in relative youth pay pushed up relative youth unemployment.[9] Since 1977 the relative pay of youths has not risen and the rise in youth unemployment reflects the general economic situation.

As we have said, the typical unemployed worker is young. He certainly does not correspond to the common image of the unemployed married man with a large family claiming lots of unemployment benefit. In fact only 50 per cent of unemployed men are married, and only 19 per cent have two or more children.[10] Thus most of them cannot possibly be social security scroungers with large families.

INDUSTRY AND REGION

We must now take a look at the industrial and regional aspects of unemployment, which are closely related. We can begin by examining the changing pattern of employees in employment (see Fig. 6). Since 1979 there has been an astounding collapse of manufacturing employment in Britain of nearly 2 million jobs— a much greater proportion than in any other major country.[11] At the same time service employment has been roughly level (falling till 1982 and then rising). So total employees in employment have fallen by 2 million.[12] Given the masculinity of manufacturing, it is not surprising that male employment has fallen by nearly 2 million, with female employment roughly constant.

The fall in manufacturing employment has hurt some areas more than others, especially the West Midlands and the North of England. Thus, unemployment has tended to rise (in terms of percentage points) in the areas which already had higher unemployment.[13]

This can be seen from Figure 7. This figure of course conceals immense variation within regions, where some towns have become industrial deserts. There are certainly streets in the North of England (let alone Northern Ireland) where half the labour force are out of work. But, taking quite large travel-to-work areas, here are some horror stories: Londonderry 29 per

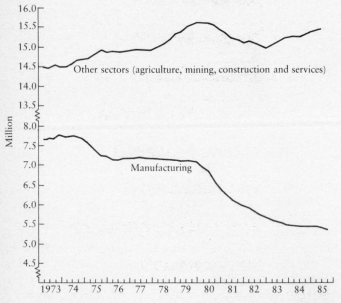

Fig. 6. Employment in manufacturing and other sectors, 1973–85.

cent, Lanarkshire 21 per cent, Merthyr 20 per cent, South Tyneside 26 per cent, Middlesbrough 23 per cent. By comparison the South can offer Crawley and Basingstoke, both at 6 per cent.[14]

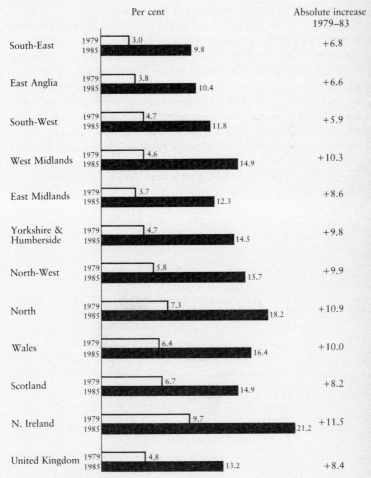

	Per cent		Absolute increase 1979–83
South-East	1979	3.0	
	1985	9.8	+6.8
East Anglia	1979	3.8	
	1985	10.4	+6.6
South-West	1979	4.7	
	1985	11.8	+5.9
West Midlands	1979	4.6	
	1985	14.9	+10.3
East Midlands	1979	3.7	
	1985	12.3	+8.6
Yorkshire & Humberside	1979	4.7	
	1985	14.5	+9.8
North-West	1979	5.8	
	1985	15.7	+9.9
North	1979	7.3	
	1985	18.2	+10.9
Wales	1979	6.4	
	1985	16.4	+10.0
Scotland	1979	6.7	
	1985	14.9	+8.2
N. Ireland	1979	9.7	
	1985	21.2	+11.5
United Kingdom	1979	4.8	
	1985	13.2	+8.4

Fig. 7. Unemployment Rates by Region, 1979 and 1985 (August)
* Post-1982 basis, excluding school leavers.

The industrial structure of unemployment (as opposed to employment) is not that clear a concept, since only 33 per cent of unemployed workers go back to the industry which they were in.[15] But if we classify the unemployed by their last job, we get the unemployment rates shown in Figure 8.

Clearly, some industries are always more unemployment-prone than others. The most obvious case is construction, where building projects are often short and workers are unemployed for a while in between projects. (This is another case where the differences in unemployment rates are mainly explained by differences in entry rates rather than duration). Having said all this, it remains the case that employment *has* fallen more in manufacturing and construction than in other sectors, and manufacturing and construction have the highest unemployment rates.[16]

THE LABOUR FORCE AND UNEMPLOYMENT

Finally, one obvious question. Can the level of unemployment be explained by the size of the labour force? As a matter of arithmetic, we know that

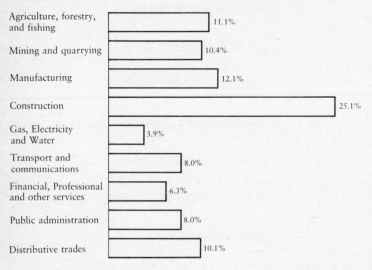

Fig. 8. Unemployment Rates by Industry, May 1982

Unemployment = Labour force − Employment.

So if the labour force were lower and employment the same, unemployment would be reduced. Later on we shall argue that over a longish run unemployment is not going to be affected by the labour force, since if the labour force rises, employment will rise. That is certainly what has happened for most of the last two hundred years. But at this stage let us just look at the facts.

In Britain the labour force grew substantially from 1950 to 1966 (see Fig. 9). Unemployment was pretty well stable. The

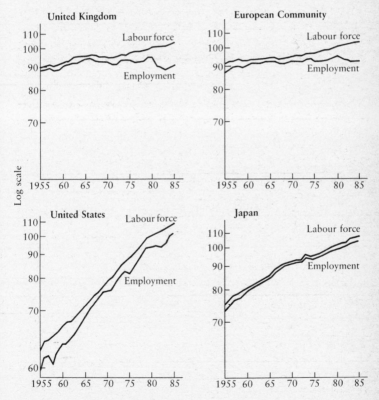

Fig. 9. Labour Force, Employment and Unemployment in UK, EEC, US and Japan (1979 Labour Force = 100).

labour force then fell for five years and then resumed its former growth (except between 1980 and 1983). Throughout the period since 1966 (of both falling *and* rising labour force), unemployment rose.

The contrast with the US and Japan is striking. In both these countries the labour force rose much more than in Britain or Europe, yet unemployment rose much less. This can be seen by comparing the slopes of the lines in Figure 9.

So why did unemployment rise so much here? It is time to make a systematic attempt to find out.

Summary

1. Since 1966, unemployment in Britain has risen in most years. The same is true of the European Community. By contrast, US unemployment has gone up and down, and is now as low as in 1980.
2. Unemployment in Britain is now as high as unemployment in 1930–34. But in the early 1930s unemployment first rose sharply and then fell sharply. Today it has been high for four years and with present policies is unlikely to fall sharply.
3. Unemployment has mainly risen through an increase in how long people remain unemployed. Today 40 per cent of the unemployed in Britain have been out of work for over a year. In the US and Sweden (where benefits are not indefinitely available), the proportion is 12 per cent.
4. Roughly half of the unemployed men were made redundant from their previous job and 10 per cent have never worked.
5. Unemployment rates are particularly high among the young, the unskilled, in construction, and in the North of England.
6. In most periods of history a rise in the labour force has led to a rise in employment, not to extra unemployment.

3

The Inflation/Unemployment Quandary

What has gone wrong? Governments do not like unemployment and it is not good for their re-election prospects. So why don't they reduce it? The answer of course is that they also dislike inflation, and so do their electorates.

The only reason we have unemployment is that governments are using it to contain, or to reduce, inflation. Generally, governments will not admit this. But if you ever suggest doing anything to expand the economy, their answer will always be, 'That's inflationary'. In fact why else would they not do something desirable like creating jobs? Clearly they *are* using unemployment to control inflation.

Thus, to understand unemployment, we need to understand the relation between unemployment and inflation, and what affects it. This chapter will be the toughest part of the book, but it is really just common sense.

INFLATION AND UNEMPLOYMENT

If unemployment is low, inflation will tend to rise. Employers will find it more difficult to fill their vacancies. So they will try to attract workers by paying more than the going rate. At the same time unions will feel in a stronger position to push for wage increases. But, if unemployment is high enough, inflation will be stable; and, if it is even higher, inflation will actually fall, as happened in the early 1980s.

Thus there is a critical level of unemployment at which inflation will be just stable—neither rising nor falling. We shall call this the NAIRU (the non-accelerating inflation rate of unemployment)—a terrible phrase but one that has somehow got established. This is charted in Figure 10. If unemployment is pushed below the NAIRU, inflation increases; and, if unemployment is

pushed above this point, inflation can be reduced. The relationship between the change in inflation and the level of unemployment is shown by the sloping line. In the example chosen, the
NAIRU is 10 per cent unemployment (or 2.5 million), which
may not be too far from the mark.[1] (This does not allow for
novel policies of the kind outlined in Chapter 1.) Starting from
the NAIRU, a 1 per cent lower level of unemployment would
make inflation rise by about 1 per cent a year—again a reasonably plausible estimate.[2]

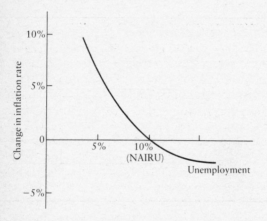

Fig. 10. Unemployment and Inflation (how inflation will rise if
unemployment is below the NAIRU, and vice versa)

One might ask why low unemployment leads to rising inflation, rather than simply to rising prices. In other words why,
when unemployment is low, do we find inflation rising, rather
than prices rising at a steady rate of inflation? The answer is that
inflation has a momentum (or inertia) of its own. If there is no
particular pressure in the labour market, people expect inflation
to continue at its former level. So if prices are already rising they
will continue to rise. Extra pressure in the labour market will
make them rise faster.

To see how reasonable this whole argument is, Figure 11
shows the history of inflation relative to unemployment. The top

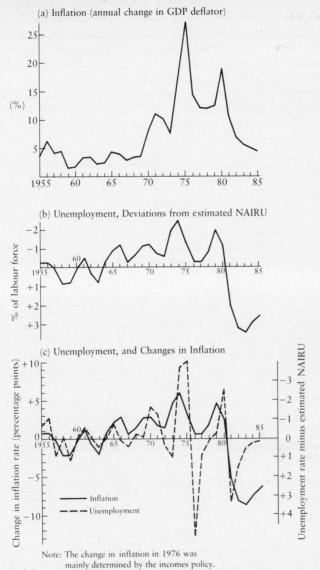

(a) Inflation (annual change in GDP deflator)

(b) Unemployment, Deviations from estimated NAIRU

(c) Unemployment, and Changes in Inflation

— Inflation
-- Unemployment

Note: The change in inflation in 1976 was
mainly determined by the incomes policy.

Fig. 11. Unemployment and Inflation in the UK, 1955–85.

panel shows the inflation rate. The next panel shows the unemployment rate adjusted for the estimated change in the NAIRU. It is shown on an inverted scale, so that peaks on the graph reflect peaks in economic activity. It is these peaks which cause inflation to increase, while troughs cause it to decrease.

Thus the final panel plots together the unemployment peaks and troughs *and* the changes in inflation. This last graph provides a potted history of the last 30 years. As can be seen, inflation tended to rise in the booms of 1956, 1961, 1965, and 1970 (all of them related to elections!). In the slacker intervening periods, inflation tended to fall (or rise less). The boom of 1973, however, had an altogether disproportionate effect on inflation. This was because it coincided with booms in most other countries, leading to an explosion of commodity prices and the accompanying first oil price rise. Matters were made much worse by the indexation arrangements embodied in the prevailing incomes policy. The passive policies of the incoming Labour government did nothing to dampen the fires of inflation, and by 1976 the situation was so critical that a drastic incomes policy (£6 a week for all, or 10 per cent for the average person) was introduced. This had a sensational effect in reducing inflation from 27 per cent in 1975 to 14 per cent the following year. The next inflationary surge came in 1979–80, following on the partial economic recovery of 1978–9 and the abandonment of the incomes policy. However this time the fire was put out by a huge dose of unemployment. This brought inflation down rapidly in 1981, and inflation since then has remained well under control. It has not however continued to fall as much as one might have expected, and we discuss the reasons for this in the next chapter.

Thus there *is* a clear relation between unemployment and inflation, but only if we recognize the fact that the NAIRU has risen.

THE RISE IN UNEMPLOYMENT

We can now come back to unemployment, and think of its rise as consisting of two parts:

(i) First there is the rise in the NAIRU, which needs to be explained in detail.

(ii) Second, there is an 'overkill' i.e. a rise in unemployment above the NAIRU (resulting in a fall in inflation).

The Overkill

Let us start with the overkill. In the short-run the level of unemployment is determined by 'aggregate demand', that is, by the demand for British output. In the last six years this demand has fallen sharply relative to our potential output. Much of the fall in demand has resulted from government policy. We shall spend the whole of Chapter 5 going over this. The fall in demand has raised unemployment by at least 5 percentage points.[3] High priority has been given to *reducing* inflation by reducing demand. Until this deflation of demand is moderated, the hopes for unemployment are poor. For the quickest way to raise employment is to spend more money now, and accept that inflation will continue at the present level. The alternative is not to boost money spending, but to rely on falling inflation to increase its real value. This takes much longer.

Factors Affecting the NAIRU

So much for the 'demand-side' factors affecting unemployment. But there is also the rise in the NAIRU, which has reduced the ability of the economy to supply extra output without this leading to extra inflation. This is what people mean when they talk about the importance of improving the 'supply-side' of the economy. They do not mean only improving the supply of labour. They mean everything which affects the ability of the economy to provide a sustained supply of output at stable inflation.

So what factors may have increased the NAIRU? There are a whole host of possible explanations.

1. The two oil price rises of 1973 and 1979.
2. The slowdown in productivity growth.
3. The rise in taxation.
4. Easier access to social security benefits.

5. More mismatch between jobs available and the qualities of the unemployed.
6. Employment protection, making it harder to sack workers once hired.
7. Increases in union militancy.
8. Finally, there is the likelihood that high unemployment in the recent past can raise the NAIRU, at least temporarily. This would help to explain why wage inflation is not now falling as much as one might expect.

All these factors must have played a role, and we shall discuss them one by one in this chapter and the next. But, before we can do this, we need some general idea about how the NAIRU is determined. We can then use this framework to look at the factors which must affect it.

HOW THE NAIRU IS DETERMINED

The theory is very simple. In a nutshell, there is at any particular time a limit to the living standards which the economy can provide to its workers. In other words there is a 'feasible' real wage. If workers try to get more than this, inflation will increase—with wages accelerating and prices following them upwards. So stable inflation requires realistic behaviour at the bargaining table.

What assures this? The answer is that there must be enough unemployment. Just enough unemployment will ensure that the 'target' real wage equals the 'feasible' real wage. If there is 'not enough' unemployment, wages will be pushed too high and wage inflation will increase. Alternatively, if there is 'excess' unemployment, wage and price inflation will fall.

To make the matter more concrete, we have to look first at how firms set prices, and then at how wage-bargainers (i.e. firms and unions) set wages. In the long run, the pricing behaviour of firms determines the real wage. For, whatever money wage is set, firms will set prices so as to bring the purchasing power of wages down to the normal level. Thus, suppose there is a normal price mark-up (of prices over wages), so that

$$Prices = Wages \times Normal\ price\ mark\text{-}up.$$

It follows that the feasible real wage is given by

$$Feasible\ real\ wage = \frac{Wages}{Prices} = \frac{1}{Normal\ price\ mark\text{-}up}.$$

This is shown as a horizontal line in Figure 12.[4]

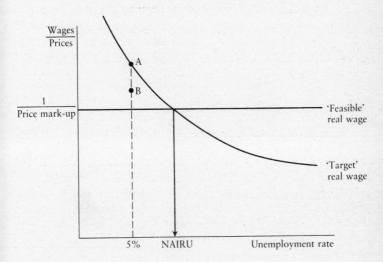

Fig. 12. How the NAIRU is determined.

The statement that the real wage is basically determined by firms may seem surprising, since money wages are determined by wage-bargainers. But in the long run the real wage which the wage-bargainers settle for must be consistent with the feasible real wage. If workers try to set wages too high relative to prices, we shall get upwards-spiralling inflation.

What eventually stops this? The answer is that the wage-bargainers eventually adjust their behaviour. For their behaviour (unlike that of price-setters) depends strongly on unemployment. If inflation is increasing, governments will allow unemployment to increase. This will dampen wage pressure and eventually consistency between the two mark-ups will be restored. Higher unemployment will reduce the target real wage until it is equal to what is feasible.

The restraining influence of unemployment on wage-bargaining is shown in the sloping line of Figure 12. At some level of unemployment there is just enough unemployment to make wage-bargainers settle on the real wage that firms are willing to deliver. That level of unemployment is the NAIRU.

Let us trace out carefully what happens if the government creates so many jobs that unemployment falls below the NAIRU—to, say, 5 per cent. Wage-bargainers push up wage inflation above expected price inflation (more, that is, than any difference due to productivity growth). Because they underestimate the rise of price inflation induced by their actions, they do not hit the real wage at A which they were aiming at, but they do get *some* increase in real wages (as at B). Firms provide this increase because they too underestimated the rise in wages, and so allowed their price mark-up over actual wages to fall. So rising inflation was the device that reconciled the behaviour of wage-bargainers and the marketing managers of firms. As James Meade has put it, rising inflation is the only possible outcome if you try to get a quart out of a pint pot. By the same token, it is only the rising inflation which made it possible for us to have more employment than at the NAIRU.

So we have now gone behind the crude assumptions of Figure 10 to see *why* inflation rises when unemployment is 'too low': it is because low unemployment encourages unrealistic wage behaviour. Equally, if unemployment is very high, the unions get cowed, wages are too low a mark-up on prices, and inflation falls.

CHANGES IN THE NAIRU

Over the century, of course, the underlying real wage has risen, and this has caused no problem since wage-bargainers have settled for increases which the economy could afford. But trouble can come from two sources. First, something can happen which reduces the feasible real wage below what might have been expected. Second, wage setters can try to push the real wage higher than is warranted. Either event will lead to an increase in the NAIRU.

The first source of trouble (a fall in the feasible real wage) is illustrated in Figure 13(a). As can be seen, this must raise unem-

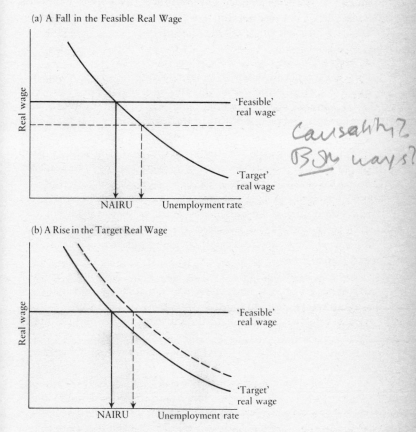

(a) A Fall in the Feasible Real Wage

Causality?
B.sh ways?

(b) A Rise in the Target Real Wage

Fig. 13. How the NAIRU can be increased.

ployment. The second source of trouble is a rise in the down-wards-sloping schedule showing the target real wage. This is illustrated in Figure 13(b) and will also create unemployment.

We can investigate any increase in the NAIRU under one or other of these headings. In this analysis we shall always use the 'real wage' to refer to the real take-home pay of workers, that is the amount of goods and services this pay will buy. This is the money wage after direct taxes, divided by the consumer price index (which is affected by indirect taxes and taxes on employers). We shall begin with the first kind of problem— events which cut the feasible real wage.

The Oil Shock

It is natural to start with the oil shock of 1973–4, which first pushed unemployment over the 1 million mark. For some years many economists thought the oil shock was the only problem, though this turned out not to be the case. However at the time it was a major problem, and gave rise to a major inflationary impulse. For if the price of imported goods goes up, the prices in the shops will have to go up at any given level of money wages. So real wages will fall.[5] Let us look at the size of this effect. At the same time as oil prices rose, the prices of other imports rose too—especially of imported food and raw materials. If we look at how all import prices affected the feasible real wage, between 1972 and 1975 they reduced it by over 5 per cent. This is shown in Figure 14(a).

Such a reduction could have only been contained without inflation if workers had taken an equivalent cut in their real wage. Perhaps not surprisingly they resisted, and inflation rose. The government then fought the inflation by preventing money national income from rising as fast as prices. So the real value of output fell (as prices outpaced money spending), and unemployment rose.

In 1979 there was another rise in oil prices and commodity prices. But what does this explain of our present unemployment? Very little. For as Figure 14(a) shows, these changes had no effect on the feasible wage. By this time Britain was no longer a net importer of oil.[6] And in any case world commodity prices

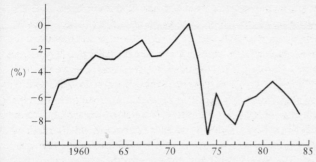

Fig. 14(a). Effect of Import Prices on the Level of the Feasible Real Wage (1972 = 0)

(excluding oil) have now fallen to record low levels (relative to prices generally).[7] So no one can use commodity prices as an excuse for unemployment any longer.

The Slowdown in Productivity Growth

The same is true of the productivity downturn. In the mid-1970s there was a marked fall in the rate of growth of output per worker. In most European countries the annual growth rate fell by about 2 percentage points. This was due partly to a fall in the rate of increase in the amount of capital per worker, but also to a fall in the rate of technical progress (i.e. the growth in the amount of output produced by a given amount of capital and labour).

This initially caused trouble on the wages front, as workers failed to accept that the growth in the feasible real wage had tailed off. In consequence unemployment had to rise to make them 'accept reality'.

But it is now 10 years since this downturn in the growth rate occurred, and there is some sign that productivity growth may be reverting towards its former levels. So a failure of adaptation of this kind can hardly explain our present unemployment.

Taxes

This brings us to a third other obvious force which could reduce the real wage—namely, tax increases. These are shown in Figure

14(b). Any tax increase will reduce real take-home pay.[8] If the tax is an indirect tax (VAT or the excise duties) or the employers' National Insurance contribution, it will reduce the real wage by raising prices (for given wages). If the tax is a direct tax (income tax or employees' National Insurance contributions), prices will be unaffected (for given wages), but take-home pay will fall.

So are higher taxes a cause of unemployment, as some Conservatives sometimes argue? Certainly the average tax rate has risen since 1970. But in econometric work it is not at all easy to find any effect on unemployment. It seems as though when taxes reduce real take-home pay, they also reduce the real wage sought by wage-bargainers by much the same amount. This is certainly true of direct and indirect taxes. It may be less true of the employers' National Insurance contributions (the hated 'jobs tax'). But this is not easy to pin down. My own view is that it is the *structure* of the employers' National Insurance contribution that we should concentrate on, rather than its *level*. But this is for later.

For the moment my conclusion is that if we want to explain the increase in the NAIRU we should focus less on forces which tended to lower the feasible real wage (just discussed) than on the forces that tended to raise the target real wage that was sought. These forces could include the social security system, employment protection, mismatch, and trade union power—all of which we discuss in the next chapter.

Summary

1. At any time there is a level of unemployment consistent with stable inflation (NAIRU). If unemployment is lower than this, inflation will tend to rise; and, if unemployment is higher, inflation will tend to fall. This is why inflation rose in the early 1970s and fell in the early 1980s.

2. The NAIRU is determined as follows. At any time there is a 'feasible' real wage that the economy 'can deliver'. Unemployment has to be high enough to make wage-bargainers settle for a 'target' real wage equal to the 'feasible' real wage. If unemployment is lower than that, wage-bargainers will go for too high a 'target' real wage. Inflation will increase, as

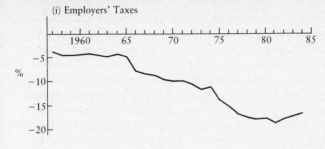

(i) Employers' Taxes

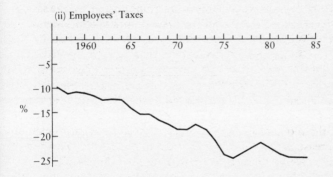

(ii) Employees' Taxes

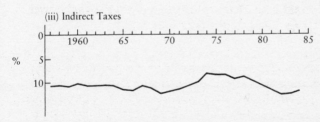

(iii) Indirect Taxes

Fig. 14(b). Effect of Taxes on the Level of the Feasible Real Wage.

prices rise faster than expected, cheating wage-bargainers of part of the real wage which they had hoped for.
3. The NAIRU will rise if, at a given level of unemployment, wage-bargainers aim at a higher target real wage relative to the feasible real wage. Problems can therefore arise from

either falls in the feasible real wage or rises in the target real wage.

4. The feasible real wage can be reduced by rises in relative import prices, by falls in productivity and by rises in taxation. After the first oil shock, the rise in import prices helped to raise the NAIRU for a time. But there is no unambiguous evidence of problems coming from the productivity slow-down or from changes in taxation; these seem to have mainly been absorbed by falls in the target real wage.

5. The target real wage can be increased due to easier social security, more employment protection, greater mismatch or stronger trade unions—all considered in the next chapter.

4

The Supply Side:
Social Security, Employment Protection,
Mismatch and Trade Unions

SOCIAL SECURITY

How far has unemployment risen because the unemployed are less willing to take work? It must be a factor. For there are today almost as many vacancies as there were in the recession of 1971. Yet unemployment is four times as high. This raises some pretty fundamental questions.

Let us first clarify the facts, which appear in Figure 15.[1] This shows for each year the proportion of men unemployed *and* the number of unfilled jobs available. As can be seen, there has been a steady and remorseless increase in the number of people unemployed at any particular level of vacancies. For example the number of vacancies was the same in 1959 and in 1979; yet unemployment was three times higher.

There has also been another important change since the 1960s: a massive fall in the number of vacancies. So we have two facts to explain. Why are more people unemployed nowadays at any particular level of vacancies, and why are there so few vacancies? For the moment we shall concentrate on the first of these.

If unemployment goes up at given vacancies, this could be due to one of three things. First, the unemployed could have become more choosey about the existing vacancies or not be looking so hard to find them. Second, there could be more mismatch between the unemployed workers and the pattern of jobs available (in terms of skill, region, and industry). Third, the employers could have become more choosey about the available unemployed workers. We shall look at these three explanations

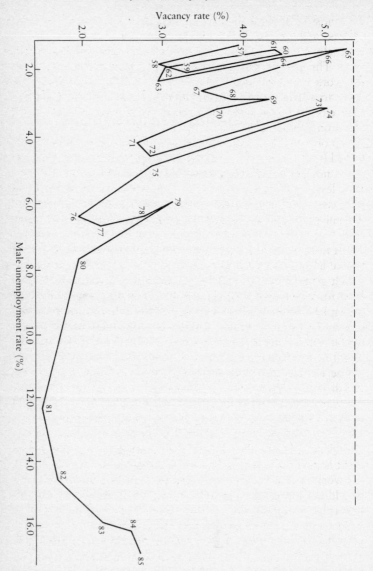

Fig. 15. Vacancies and Male Unemployment.

in turn, starting with the first.

This says essentially that the unemployed have become more work-shy (when there is any particular number of jobs available). There could of course have been a spontaneous change in the work ethic, but most people would link it in some way or other to changes in the availability of social security. So let us look closely at the possible ways in which social security can affect unemployment.

It is obvious that if there were no social security, more people would be at work. For, if the jobless got no income, people who could not get work they like would be forced to do work they liked less. This is what happens in poor countries. People who do not have regular jobs take casual work (often part time), or become self-employed as petty traders, shoe-shine boys, or whatever.

But most of us, if we lost our jobs, would not like to be forced to live like that. So it makes sense to have an insurance scheme which gives unemployed workers enough to live on while they look for other work. We know that such a scheme will make unemployed people more choosey about what work they will seek and how far from their homes they will look. But we accept that it is fair for people who suffer misfortune to be protected, and it is what we would wish for ourselves.

The issue is the exact scale of protection, and the terms on which it is available. Before looking at these in detail, let me forewarn you of my conclusions. The evidence suggests that at current levels of benefits, a 10 per cent cut in benefits would only reduce unemployment by about 5 per cent of its current level— not worth contemplating. But it also suggests that unemployment is much affected by how hard people are expected to look for work, and what kind of work they can be expected to take. In addition, long-term unemployment would be much less if, as Beveridge proposed, normal benefits had a limited duration.

So what are the facts? At present in Britain an unemployed person gets a flat-rate Unemployment Benefit for 12 months as of right if the basic conditions are satisfied. If the person has children, Child Benefit will also be coming in.[2] Even so, it is quite possible that the income which is provided in this way will be less than the minimum income which the state guarantees the unemployed through Supplementary Benefit. This pays a basic scale-rate plus housing costs.[3] Table 4 shows Supplementary Benefit plus typical housing costs for an unemployed person. As the table shows, Supplementary Benefit is generally higher than Unemployment Benefit, so that a family which has no other source of income than Unemployment Benefit can have it topped up to the Supplementary Benefit level. About one in four of those on Unemployment Benefit in fact receives Supplementary Benefit as well.

After one year's unemployment, a person can no longer get Unemployment Benefit, but Supplementary Benefit is available indefinitely, provided the person remains available for work. Thus Supplementary Benefit is more important than Unemployment Benefit in determining the living standards of the unemployed.[4]

An obvious question is how Supplementary Benefit compares with the incomes which the unemployed can expect in work. This is a very complicated question. As a benchmark, Table 4 also shows the after-tax earnings of each type of family if it had one earner only, receiving the average earnings for a man in that family type. The next column shows for each type of family the disposable income (excluding housing costs) when unemployed relative to spendable income in work. This is an example of a 'replacement ratio' i.e. the ratio of the replacement income (while unemployed) to the normal income (when in work). It is in this case a notional figure relevant only to a family on average earnings.

As can be seen, this notional replacement ratio is a lot more favourable for people in large families. This has given rise to the image of the social security scrounger with lots of children. But, as column (5) shows, the typical unemployed person has no children at all. If we want to compute a standardized notional replacement ratio, we have to weight the ratios for each family type by the proportion of the unemployed in each family type. This gives an overall ratio of 46 per cent.

All of this is calculated on the basis that the household includes only one earner earning the average earnings of a man

Table 4. Comparison of Incomes In and Out of Work, January 1986 (single earner on average male manual earnings)

Family type	Unemployment Benefit plus Child Benefit (£ p.w.) (1)	Supplementary benefit		After-tax income (£ p.w.) (4)	Replacement ratios % (5)=(2)/ [(4)−(3)]	Male unemployed in this family type % (6)
		Scale rate (£ p.w.) (2)	+ Housing costs (£ p.w.) (3)			
Single	30.45	29.50 +	19.05	97.40	38	51
Married no children	49.25	47.85 +	19.05	119.70	48	20
Married, 1 child	56.25	57.95 +	21.65	132.50	52	10
Married, 2 children	63.25	68.05 +	22.95	139.50	58	10
Married. 3 children	70.25	78.15 +	22.95	146.50	63	6
Married, 4 children	77.25	93.25 +	22.05	153.50	71	3
Weighted average					46	100

Note:
For single people the above rates relate to householders. For non-householders the scale rate is £23.60 plus £3.90 notional housing costs. Joint-householders (such as people who share a flat) get between £23.60 and £29.50, depending on the size of household, plus their housing costs. Non-householders and joint-householders are four-fifths of the total of single men who become unemployed, but a lower proportion of the stock of unemployed single men.

in that type of family. In practice, the majority of wives under 60 work (roughly 25 per cent full time and 31 per cent part time).[5] As against this, the unemployed are drawn largely from people paid less than average earnings. Thus while calculations like those we have just done are the best we can do when studying changes over time, we do want something better to understand the present situation.

Fortunately this is possible for recent years. The DHSS cohort study of the unemployed showed the weekly income of families including an unemployed man and compared this with the same family's income before unemployment began.[6] There were a few families which were actually better off while unemployed, as Table 5 shows—but very few.These figures reflect of course the mixture of Unemployment Benefit and Supplementary Benefit that these families actually got. The table makes clear that most families suffer a substantial income loss when one of their members becomes unemployed. The typical family loses nearly half its income.

Table 5. Income While Unemployed as a Proportion of Family Income Before Unemployment (men, 1982)

Replacement ratio	Per cent
Over 100%	3
80%–100%	18
50%–80%	40
Under 50%	39
	100

There are of course some expenses of working (clothing and travel) which could be subtracted before computing income in work. Since these are about 5 per cent of income in work, deducting them would raise the replacement ratio on average by about 2 percentage points.[7] Even after this, there are very few people who would be financially better off if they did not work. But in any case this number is not that crucial. Many people are willing to work for nothing—in hospitals, clubs, and voluntary associations. Equally, many other people would not be willing to work, even if it made them 30 per cent better off. So, while we are very interested in replacement ratios, we are not particularly concerned about exactly how many unemployed people are better off or worse off than they would be in work.

The next step is to see how replacement ratios have altered over time, concentrating on Supplementary Benefit as the key part of the system. For this purpose we show in Figure 16 a notional replacement ratio of the kind we computed in Table 4, but even cruder. The index now assumes that the earner in each type of family earned the overall average male manual earnings. As it shows, the system became a lot more generous between the mid '50s and 1967. But since then Supplementary Benefits have not improved, relative to income in work. (Moreover, Earnings-Related Unemployment Benefit was abolished in 1982, and had formerly been received by 16 per cent of the unemployed.)

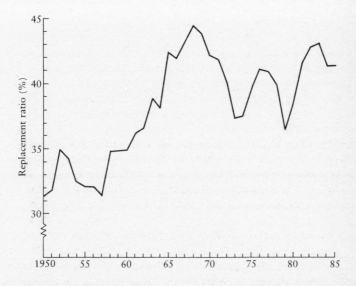

Fig. 16. The Ratio of Incomes In and Out of Work (Replacement Ratio), 1950–85.

So how much of our higher unemployment can be explained by changes in social security benefits? Since the replacement ratio has not risen since the mid '60s, the obvious answer is, Not much. But there are two possible qualifications to this, which should be considered. First, unemployment may depend not only on the ratio of benefits to income in work but also on the real level of benefits. The latter has of course risen since 1966, roughly in line with real net earnings. If this argument is right, richer societies (with a given replacement ratio) will tend to have more unemployment than poorer societies (with the same replacement ratio). This would imply that unemployment should have been rising for the last 150 years, which we do not see. So we can ignore this argument.

Second, it could take time (and especially a depression) for people to realize that benefits are now more generous. In this case there might be delayed effects of the changes that happened in the 1960s. One cannot rule out the possibility that these effects ran on well into the 1970s.

But how big could the effects have been? How can we learn about this? One approach is to put the replacement ratio in with other factors into a statistical analysis of the time series. Unfortunately it is difficult to disentangle the effects this way.[8] An alternative approach is to compare the behaviour of unemployed people facing different replacement ratios. The work of Stephen Nickell suggests that if a man has a 10 per cent higher replacement ratio his unemployment is likely to last about 5 per cent longer. Thus a 50 per cent rise in the replacement ratio (as happened from the mid '50s to 1967) could raise unemployment by at most a quarter.[9] This clearly does not explain most of the six-fold rise in unemployment since the early 1960s.

THE ADMINISTRATION OF BENEFITS

So much for the effect of the level of benefits. But what about the terms on which they are available? This is the issue of the test of 'willingness to work', known for short as the 'work test'. At one extreme people could be allowed to draw benefit at will, if they decided not to work. At the other extreme, they might be denied benefit unless they are willing to take work of any kind that is available within, say 25 miles of their homes. In fact our system operates somewhere in between these extremes. People are in principle not allowed to get benefit unless they are available for work, and willing to accept suitable work that comes along. But there has been a progressive reduction in the severity of the 'work test', as measured by the pressure placed upon claimants to find work.

This has been going on for many years, beginning long before the mass unemployment of the 1980s. Table 6 gives some evidence on the denial of benefit. If a person on Unemployment Benefit refuses an offer of suitable employment or 'neglects to avail' of work opportunities that exist, the employment service can refer his case to an insurance officer.[10] If the officer accepts the charge, then (subject to appeal) the person loses his Unemployment Benefit for up to six weeks. As the table shows, the numbers referred fell steadily up to 1973, after which they fell precipitously. In addition, from 1974 onwards there was a sharp fall in the proportion of all referred people who were eventually refused benefit.

People can also be refused Unemployment Benefit for up to six weeks if they left their previous job. In practice this provision does not seem to be used to the full. In 1981, 17 per cent of the unemployed had resigned from their previous job and about 5 per cent of new claimants were refused benefit.

A person who is disqualified from Unemployment Benefit can still get some Supplementary Benefit. Normally any individual whose income is below the national minimum gets Supplementary Benefit sufficient to raise him to the minimum. But, if he has been disqualified from Unemployment Benefit, he normally loses 40 per cent of the personal scale-rate of Supplementary Benefit for up to six weeks (though his dependents' benefits and rent are paid in full). If the person continues to refuse work, he can eventually be prosecuted for failing to maintain himself and his family. Prosecutions raise obvious difficulties and the number of

Table 6. Harrassment of the Work-Shy (Unemployed people refusing suitable employment or 'neglecting to avail')

	Number referred to Insurance Officer (1)	Percentage of column (1) denied benefit (2)
1968	29 300	78
1969	26 500	78
1970	25 200	79
1971	20 500	79
1972	21 700	79
1973	20 000	83
1974	13 800	82
1975	7 200	73
1976	5 900	68
1977	8 600	69
1978	7 900	64
1979	13 100	61
1980	16 000	58
1981	10 700	46
1982	7 000	39
1983	6 100	32

prosecutions has fallen from around 100 a year in the 1960s to under 10.

So what explains the trends shown in the table? They probably reflect, above all, profound changes in social attitudes towards people receiving public money. The most glaring example of this was the altogether new phenomenon in the 1970s of large numbers of full-time students on vacation receiving benefits designed for the 'unemployed'. But in addition there has been an interesting set of institutional changes in Britain since 1973 which may have further encouraged the tendencies at work.

Until 1973, benefit was paid out in the same office where people were found jobs (i.e. the employment exchange). The two operations were seen as part of the same process—to maintain a person's living standard while trying to get him back to work. Between 1973 and about 1977 these functions were split, with separate Job Centres (for job placement) and benefit offices (for paying benefit). The payout of benefit became more automatic, with less effort made to find a job for those who had been receiving benefit for too long.

Until 1982 benefit recipients had to register at Job Centres, but then even this requirement was abolished. At about the same time signing on at the benefit office was changed from once a week to once a fortnight. The erosion of the work test has gone a long way.

All of this is of course a different issue from social security fraud, when an unemployed person is secretly working. Little is known about this. In 1981 the official Rayner Committee estimated that at least 8 per cent of those on benefit had undisclosed work (often of course part time), while 16 per cent were not seeking work.[11] Most of those involved in fraud probably have fairly unproductive jobs and it would be better if they, like the 'work-shy', were more actively seeking for solid work. For this would reduce the degree of wage pressure at a given unemployment, and thus make it possible to run the economy with less unemployment.

SPECIAL PROBLEM OF THE LONG-TERM UNEMPLOYED

This raises another important issue. There is clear evidence that the long-term unemployed are less actively searching for work than those who lost their job more recently. The Department of Health and Social Security study of a cohort of the unemployed showed that people who had been out of work for more than a year spent less time and less money looking for work. They have also lost their skills and become less attractive to employers. For all these reasons one would expect that at any given level of total unemployment, there would be more vacancies the higher the fraction of the unemployed who had been out of work for over a year. Or, to put it another way, at given vacancies, there would be more unemployment. This turns out to be true. In fact much of the increase in unemployment at given vacancies since 1979 can be explained by the increase in the proportion of the long-term unemployed.

Given this, one could expect that the long-term unemployed would exert less downwards pressure on wages than the short-term unemployed. It turns out that they exert no downwards pressure whatsoever.[12] Since the only point of unemployment is to control inflation, this suggests that long-term unemployment is a complete waste.

It therefore becomes easier to understand why wage inflation has not been falling in the last three years. The extra long-term unemployed are simply doing nothing in the fight against inflation. They have largely withdrawn from the labour force.

A different interpretation of why only short-term unemployment matters is that it is high when employed people are most likely to lose their jobs. On this interpretation wages are restrained by the fear of job loss, rather than by the number of job-seekers with whom an employed person would have to compete if he lost his job.

Either way the development of unemployment since 1981 is particularly tragic. For since then the number of people unemployed for under a year has actually fallen, as Figure 4 shows. The whole increase has been of people unemployed over a year.

This in turn leads one to ask why long-term unemployment has increased. A purely arithmetical answer is as follows. When unemployment went up between 1980 and 1982, the number of people who became unemployed rose much less than in proportion. The main rise came through an increase in duration, as employers failed to hire the same proportion of the unemployed as in earlier years. Thus a downwards shock led to a big and seemingly permanent growth in long-term unemployment. On the demand side, employers were not keen to hire people who had been out of work so long and whose skills and work attitudes may have wasted. On the supply side, the benefit system was there to provide some cushion, so that the long-term unemployed were not forced back to menial work, as in the US, by sheer necessity. We thus have a practical explanation of today's high NAIRU in terms of the interaction of the benefit system with the severe downwards shocks administered to the economy between 1980 and 1982.

This argument is one of many which argue that the NAIRU depends in the short run on the levels of unemployment in the recent past. While econometric work is ambiguous on this issue, it probably has some truth in it.[13] It does not mean that the

NAIRU can be pushed indefinitely to any level you like (high or low) simply by pushing the economy around. But it does mean that if the economy is subjected to a downwards shock (by for example an oil price rise or by budget cuts), then for some years the level of unemployment consistent with non-accelerating inflation will be higher than the long-run NAIRU. Unemployment can only be pushed back to the long-run NAIRU without extra inflation by a gradual process—unless some extra anti-inflationary device is used, such as a temporary incomes policy.[14]

We can now revert to our original question: Why has unemployment grown so fast at given vacancies? We have established that in recent years it is associated with the growth of long-term unemployment, and in general it could be due to workers becoming more choosey about jobs. But might it not equally well be due to greater mismatch (between unemployed workers and the jobs available), or to greater choosiness on the part of employers? Let us examine these in turn.

MISMATCH BETWEEN UNEMPLOYED WORKERS AND JOBS AVAILABLE

It is often said that we live in a period of unprecedented structural change, and that this is the cause of higher unemployment. This is certainly a theoretical possibility. For suppose there is a big switch in the demand for labour from one industry to another, or from one skill to another (e.g. from skilled to unskilled), with the total demand for labour unchanged. This would create unemployment in the declining sectors, until the workers then redeployed themselves. At the same time there would be unfilled vacancies in the expanding sectors. But this is clearly not an accurate description of the shift from the 1960s to the 1980s as shown in Figure 15. For while unemployment has risen, vacancies have fallen. This means that the relative demand for labour has fallen.[15] But it is still theoretically possible that, against that background, shifts in the structure of labour demand have pushed up the level of unemployment at any particular level of vacancies.

Does the evidence support this idea? The answer is No. To investigate this, we need to break the unemployed down between sectors and see how well they are matched to the vacancies (also broken down between sectors). A perfect match would be if the breakdown of vacancies was the same as the breakdown of the unemployed. This is illustrated in Figure 17—splitting the labour force for simplicity into two categories of skill. In the top panel there is a perfect match, with unskilled four times as numerous as skilled among both vacancies and unemployed. In the bottom panel, there is an imperfect match, with unskilled four times as numerous among the vacancies. We can construct an index by taking for each sector the (absolute) difference between the proportion of vacancies falling in the sector and the proportion of the unemployed doing so, and then summing across sectors. Thus in the first case we get (in percentages) $(20 - 20) + (80 - 80)$, i.e. zero. In the second case we get $(80 - 20) + (80 - 20)$, i.e. 120. If we then divide this by 2 we have an index which shows what percentage of the unemployed would need to move from one sector to another in order to bring about a perfect match. In the latter case this is 60 per cent of the unemployed.[16]

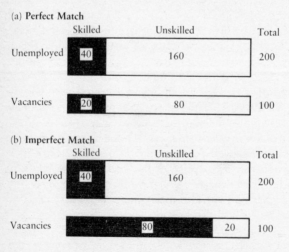

Fig. 17. The Match of Unemployment and Vacancies.

To study actual mismatch we obviously need to break the labour force down into as many categories as possible. The data let one do it for 18 occupations, for 9 regions, and 24 industrial sectors. This is shown in Table 7. As can be seen, there is no evidence of a rising trend of mismatch. It is true that industrial mismatch was high in 1981 and 1982, but this probably reflects a short-run situation rather than a change in the underlying trend.

Before going any further, let me correct one possible misinterpretation. I am not saying that mismatch is not a powerful cause of unemployment. It always has been, and it is such a serious problem that I shall be devoting a whole chapter to the question

Table 7. More Structural Unemployment? (Great Britain)

	Mismatch of unemployment and vacancies (%)			Annual percentage change in employment structure (5-year moving average)	
	By occupation	By region	By industry	By industry	By region
1963	39	31	28	2.0	0.52
1964	42	35	25	2.0	0.47
1965	41	31	24	2.1	0.43
1966	42	28	24	2.1	0.40
1967	37	28	27	2.0	0.41
1968	38	31	27	2.3	0.38
1969	39	31	29	2.4	0.47
1970	38	26	27	2.6	0.50
1971	37	27	27	2.7	0.56
1972	37	32	25	2.7	0.62
1973	40	33	23	2.7	0.64
1974	41	30	25	2.7	0.66
1975	43	20	26	2.2	0.67
1976	38	17	23	1.9	0.52
1977	35	20	21	2.0	0.49
1978	35	25	21	2.0	0.49
1979	35	26	21	2.3	0.59
1980	37	27	27	2.6	0.70
1981	41	19	35	2.9	0.78
1982	37	20	33	2.8	
1983		14		2.7	
1984		16			

of training and other structural problems. But the evidence certainly suggests that it is not a greater problem than in the past.[17]

But, you might say, surely the pace of change has been hotting up? This must cause more problems than in the past. We can investigate this directly by looking at changes in the pattern of employment. These do not, of course, exactly measure shifts in the pattern of demand for labour since there are some supply bottlenecks. But over time the scale of the changes in employment must be related to the scale of the changes in the pattern of labour demand, unless there has been some marked reduction in the responsiveness of the system.

So what can we say about the pace with which the pattern of employment is changing? Once again we can break the economy down by industry and region, and produce an index of the percentage of jobs shifting from one sector to another each year. This is also done in Table 7, which gives the 5-year moving average of these annual changes. (For example the figure shown for 1982 is the average of the annual change in 1980, 1981, 1982, 1983, and 1984.) Once again we have the picture of no increases in the pace of industrial change over what it was in the early 1970s. There was some increase in the pace of regional change, but this was probably more a result of the prolonged recession than a cause of it.

It is easy to forget the enormous industrial changes of the 1950s and 1960s. Remember the halving of mining employment in the 1960s, and the rapid decline in textiles and agriculture? These certainly caused problems, and our problems are not of a different order. We should not accept the myth that things are bound to get ever more difficult, due to the ever-increasing pace of change. They have not in the US, and we have no clear evidence either in Britain or elsewhere in Europe that this is a source of our special problems.

EMPLOYMENT PROTECTION

So we can rule out increasing mismatch as an important reason for the rise of unemployment at any particular level of vacancies.

This leaves us with two possibilities: increasing choosiness on the part of workers (already discussed), and increasing choosiness on the part of firms. One obvious reason why firms might have become more choosey is employment protection legislation. From 1966 there have been a series of laws, all making it more costly for firms to get rid of workers. This naturally makes them more cautious in taking on new workers.

There have been three main changes. The Redundancy Payments Act of 1965 introduced a statutory payment when a worker is made redundant, a part of which is a direct cost to the employer. The Industrial Relations Act of 1971 established legal rights against unfair dismissal. The Employment Protection Act of 1975 extended the periods of notice required before a redundancy.

However, the effect of employment protection upon unemployment is not at all clear-cut. For it not only discourages hirings; it also discourages sackings. Let us start with the sackings. We do not have good data on this, but we do know that the total number of separations (which includes firings plus quits) has fallen dramatically in the last 15 years.[18] This decline is a general tendency in Europe, though not in the US, and must reflect either employment protection or the general worsening of job opportunities. Now a decline in turnover should (other things equal) lead to *lower* unemployment at any particular level of vacancies, since there is less matching to be done in the labour market. Since fewer hirings are needed, the pool of unemployed people does not need to be so high.

However, this only applies other things equal. We now have to consider the willingness of firms to fill the vacancies. If it is difficult or costly to get rid of workers once you hire them, you will be much more careful who you hire. This means that more unemployed people are needed to bring about any particular number of hirings.

The net effect of these two forces upon the level of unemployment is ambiguous. I am inclined to think that they just about cancel out. I base this partly on the evidence that few employers say they would increase employment if it were easier to fire workers.[19]

Thus we have examined three possible explanations for why unemployment has grown at any particular level of vacancies. We have produced good evidence against the mismatch explanation, and we have placed a question mark over the employment protection explanation. By a process of elimination this leaves us placing the greatest weight on the view that workers have become more choosey about such jobs as are available.[20] The latter explanation is especially plausible because of the evidence that it is partly connected with the growth of long-term unemployment relative to the total unemployed.

There remains the question as to why so many fewer job vacancies are now available compared with the average of the period up to 1974. There are two elements in this: a 'trend' decline, and elements connected with 'overkill'. Both of these involve a rise in unemployment and a simultaneous fall in vacancies. We are leaving overkill to the next chapter. An obvious factor which might explain the 'trend' decline in job vacancies is the activities of unions.

UNION POWER

As we have explained, the fundamental cause of unemployment is wage pressure. Unemployment has to be high enough to contain this, except in so far as inflation is allowed to increase. The factors we have already discussed are all sources of wage pressure—they reduce the effective supply of labour associated with a given unemployment, and thereby put upwards pressure on wages. This result would follow whether wages were set unilaterally by firms, which is so in the small firms sector, or by bargaining with unions, which is so in most large firms.

In the bargaining context the outcome obviously depends not only on the balance between labour supply and demand, but also on how hard the unions push and how strong they are (for any given balance of supply and demand). How hard unions push will depend on how much they care about wages relative to employment. For if a union pushes up the relative wage in its firm, it knows that there will be fewer jobs in that firm. Many observers believe that the unions have increased the value they place on wages relative to employment. If so, this would add to wage push, as would an increase in union strength.

It is not easy to measure union objectives nor union strength. However one measure which should reflect both is the extent to which trade union wages exceed the wages of non-unionists. Figure 18 shows one estimate of this. The figure relates to the wage differential for workers covered by collective agreements (other personal characteristics being held constant). From the mid-1950s to about 1967, the 'mark-up' of trade union over other wages was fairly stable. Following the Paris riots of 1968 it rose steadily till about 1972. Then it was stable for some years until it rose again to a new plateau from 1980 onwards.

A wage explosion from 1968 was in fact a feature in nearly all European countries, and here we have a possible partial explanation of the rise in underlying unemployment between the mid-1960s and the early 1970s in Britain. Clearly many forces were at work—the end of deference and so on. But they exerted their influences through the trade union movement, and it is helpful that we have some concrete evidence of this from the figures of the trade union mark-up. The record of industrial disputes (measured by numbers of workers involved) also shows a similar change of level around the late 1960s (see Fig. 18). These changes in union activity must therefore be one reason why the British NAIRU had risen even before the first oil shock.

It is also interesting to look at the history of trade union membership. The more members unions have, the more important they are, other things equal. Here there is a striking contrast between Britain and Europe, on the one hand, and the US on the other. In the 1970s there was a surge in membership in most European countries, but a decline in the US.[21] If Europe now has more employment problems than the US, it is difficult to suppose that trends in union power have nothing to do with it.

Once again (as with the problems of job search) it is important to be clear why union objectives might have been changed since 1979 towards a higher emphasis on wages relative to employment. One approach is to say there was simply a spontaneous shift in attitudes. Another approach argues as follows. Unions care only about the employment prospects of 'insiders' i.e. those

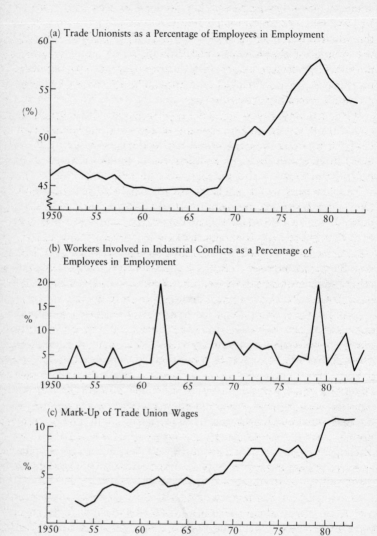

Fig. 18. Trade Unions

who are currently employed. They do not care about 'outsiders'. In 1980 and 1981 the number of insiders was much reduced by the downwards shock to employment. This presumably reduced the number of people whose employment was a concern to the unions. The unions could therefore afford to push more strongly on wages at a given level of unemployment, unbothered by the growth in the number of 'outsiders'.

If this argument were true, the reverse would also be true. A once-for-all *cut* in unemployment would tend to reduce the NAIRU, by increasing the number of insiders. If such a fall in unemployment were accompanied by a temporary incomes policy, it need not even have any affect on inflation.

This line of thought represents an extreme version of 'hysteresis'—in which the current value of a variable (here the NAIRU) depends entirely on history, and, once disturbed, has no tendency to return to any particular level. The evidence is not strong enough to make one accept the argument in its entire form.[22] For one thing it would then be difficult to see why the unemployment rate has not grown steadily over the decades, as the labour force has grown. Why did the outsiders ever get employed?

But in the short run, it must be true that the level of unemployment consistent with stable inflation *is* affected by recent unemployment. We have seen how high unemployment has increased the number of long-term unemployed, and thus reduced the average intensity of job search among the unemployed. At the same time the fall in employment may have encouraged unions to push more strongly on wages than they would otherwise have done at given unemployment. Thus even if wage inflation is not now falling, we should not think that the NAIRU could not be altered by judicious action on the demand side, though, as we shall see in Part II, the inflationary aspect of the transition would need to be carefully handled.

So what have we learned? During the late 1960s and the 1970s, access to social security became easier. This helped to raise the NAIRU. At the same time union power led to wage pressure, with the same effect. But since 1979 there has been a massive deflation of demand. This has led to a huge increase in long-term unemployment, which shows no tendency to fall.

Since long-term unemployment exerts little moderating influence on wages, wage inflation remains remarkably stable. Though this may indicate a high NAIRU, the original source of the problem is the demand deflation. We therefore turn now to the determinants of aggregate demand.

Summary

1. The unemployment rate today is four times higher than in 1971, but the number of vacancies is the same.
2. This is mainly because unemployed workers have become more choosey about taking such jobs as are available. In recent years the high proportion of long-term unemployed people helps to explain the coexistence of high unemployment and vacancies. The long-term unemployed have become demoralized and do less job search than those who have recently lost their jobs. They have also lost skills and are unattractive to employers. Long-term unemployment does nothing to restrain inflation.
3. The level of benefits has only a small effect on the level of unemployment, and a 10 per cent cut in unemployment benefits would reduce unemployment by only around 200,000. More important are the terms on which benefit is available. During the 1960s and 1970s the requirement that people on benefit be genuinely looking for work was less and less strictly applied. The NAIRU now is high partly because, when employment fell in 1980 and 1981, the open-ended benefit system made it easy for long-term unemployment to soar.
4. Employment protection has steadily reduced the turnover in the economy. But the views of employers questioned suggest that it does not account for a large proportion of the increase in the NAIRU.
5. Unemployed workers are no worse matched to the vacancies available than in earlier years. This is so whether workers and jobs are analysed in terms of occupation and regions. The rate of change of industrial structure today is no higher than in the early 1970s.
6. The power of unions has contributed to the rise in unemploy-

ment. The mark-up of union over non-union wages increased in the early 1970s and again in the early 1980s. In the early 1970s it may have reflected an increase in trade union membership and muscle. In the early 1980s it may have reflected the fact that employment fell in 1980 and 1981, and thereafter unions only cared about the welfare of the remaining 'insiders'. They thus gave a higher priority to wages relative to employment.

7. Today's high NAIRU is partly the result of the falls in employment in 1980 and 1981. With careful policies the NAIRU can be reduced.

5

Aggregate Demand

In the long run, the output of the economy is determined by the NAIRU. This constrains the output which can be *supplied* without inflation increasing. Thus in the long run (with inflation steady), the *demand* for output has to adjust to the supply. But in the short run, as we have seen, unemployment can differ widely from the NAIRU, and is then determined by the total demand for output.

In 1980 and 1981 real aggregate demand fell altogether by 5 per cent (see Fig. 19). Since 1981 output has been growing, but it has not grown fast enough to reduce unemployment. In this sense there has been no 'recovery'. Instead, there has been a roughly constant gap between actual output and the potential output of the economy. It is of course difficult to devise an unambiguous measure of potential output, but it seems reasonable to think in terms of a 2 per cent rate of growth of non-oil output from 1979.[1] This is shown in Figure 19. By this standard we are now 7 per cent below potential output.

Output is low because the aggregate demand for it is low. So what has been holding down aggregate demand? There have been two basic influences. First, the government has raised the share of taxes in national income by $4\frac{1}{2}$ percentage points. Second, our competitiveness has been eroded due to the high level of the pound in the foreign exchange market. To see why these factors matter, let us go systematically through the various components of aggregate demand, seeing how they are determined.

The constituents of demand are:

Aggregate demand = Private consumption spending
+ Public expenditure on goods
and services
+ Private investment in real capital
+ Exports − Imports.[2]

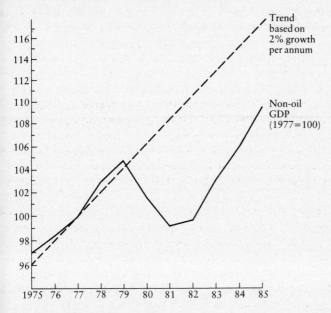

Fig. 19. The 'Output Gap'.

To understand aggregate demand, we need to review what determines each of these elements.

PRIVATE CONSUMPTION SPENDING

Starting with private consumption spending, this is much affected by the levels of tax and transfer payments (such as pensions, unemployment benefit, etc.), for consumption spending depends on the income which households have to dispose of. This 'disposable income' consists of the total income produced in the economy minus what is kept by firms as profit or by government as taxes, plus the transfers made by government.

Disposable income = Total income
− Profits retained by companies
− Taxes
+ Transfers

So to look at the impact of the budget upon activity, we can look first at the history of tax rates. As Table 8 shows, taxes have shot up since 1979 from 34 to nearly 39 per cent of income. Increased revenue from the taxation of North Sea Oil accounts for only a small proportion of this growth, and the tax rate on the non-oil economy has risen by about 3 percentage points.[3] It is striking that a government that came to power pledged to cut taxes has in fact increased them. That is a part of our problem of low aggregate demand.

Table 8. Factors Affecting Aggregate Demand, 1970–85

	Government Expenditure as % of potential output			
Taxes as % of GDP at market prices (1)	Real transfers (2)	Goods and services (3)	Real short-term interest rate (4)	IMF index of relative unit normal labour costs (5)
1970 37.1	11.4	22.6	−0.9	110
1971 35.0	10.7	22.7	−4.5	115
1972 33.5	11.9	22.9	0.9	114
1973 32.6	12.3	24.8	2.2	102
1974 35.7	12.2	26.0	−7.9	103
1975 36.2	11.4	26.4	−14.0	112
1976 35.2	11.5	26.0	−1.1	102
1977 34.8	13.1	23.5	−5.7	100
1978 33.6	14.0	22.9	3.5	108
1979 34.4	14.4	22.5	−0.7	125
1980 35.7	13.7	22.8	−1.5	152
1981 37.6	14.4	21.8	3.4	159
1982 38.6	15.2	21.5	4.6	153
1983 38.3	15.7	22.0	3.9	144
1984 38.7	16.1	21.9	4.7	143
1985			5.1	144

Private consumption spending is also affected by the welfare benefits and other transfers made from the government to private households and firms. A part of this (the payments to the unemployed) rises and falls with the level of aggregate demand. It cannot therefore be used to explain aggregate demand. So we leave this out of column (2), but include all other transfers, especially those to pensioners. We include only real interest payments on the public debt since the rest of interest payments are just compensation for the loss of private wealth due to inflation, and do not therefore stimulate spending. In column (2), transfers (thus defined) are expressed as a proportion of potential national income. As we can see, they grew sharply up to 1979 but have grown by only 1.7 points since then.

PUBLIC EXPENDITURE ON GOODS AND SERVICES

We have dealt so far with taxes and transfer payments. The rest of the budget consists of public expenditure on goods and services—education, health, defence, public administration, and so on. Column (3) compares these with potential output.[4] As we can see, expenditure has fallen by about 0.5 points since 1979.

Thus if we take together all elements of the budget (taxes, transfers, and expenditure on goods and services), their net contribution relative to GNP has fallen, since tax rates have increased by $4\frac{1}{2}$ points and expenditure by 1 point. The impact on activity has thus been severely contractionary, with a particularly massive contraction in 1981.

PRIVATE INVESTMENT

We can now look at the forces affecting the other elements of spending—private investment and exports-minus-imports. Private fixed investment means real spending on plant, machinery, vehicles, buildings, and so on. About a quarter of it is new houses. It does not mean buying stocks and shares. Private fixed investment is now much lower as a proportion of potential national income than is desirable. The average percentages relative to potential GNP have been

1970–4	12.0
1975–9	12.2
1980–4	11.5
1984	11.9

The major determinants of business investment are prospective output (which is what we have to explain), and the real rate of interest (i.e. the actual rate of interest minus expected inflation). Until recently it has been difficult to infer people's expectations of inflation,[5] but these are not likely to be far wrong for one year ahead. So, for simplicity, we show in column (4) the short-term real rate of interest, computed as the actual short-term interest rate minus the actual rate of inflation over the year. As can be seen, these rates have been very high in the 1980s compared with the 1970s. This is a world-wide phenomenon, and basically reflects the world's mix of relatively tight money and not-so-tight budgetary policy (remember the US deficit?). An individual country such as Britain has only a limited influence on its real interest rate, for, if the rate goes too low, money invested here will simply want to go abroad, causing an exchange rate crisis. However domestic monetary policy can have *some* effect.

BALANCE OF TRADE

Finally, we come to the all-important balance of trade, using this to mean exports minus imports (including goods *and* services). This depends on three main forces. First there is our competitiveness, meaning the price of foreign goods relative to our own. As Figure 20 shows, this has been much lower in the 1980s than in the 1970s, with disastrous implications for the performance of our manufacturing sector.[6] Next there is world trade, which has also been low relative to trend—with again bad effects on our exports. Finally there is domestic income (which is what we are trying to explain).

So how is competitiveness determined? It depends of course on both British and foreign price levels (in national currencies), but also on the exchange rate. In fact, exchange rate fluctuations are the main source of fluctuations in competitiveness. If the value of our currency rises, our competitiveness falls. For example, between 1978 and 1980, the pound rose from $1.92 to $2.33 to the pound. Other things equal this would have reduced our competitiveness by 18 per cent. In fact, because of price movements and other exchange rate changes, our competitive-

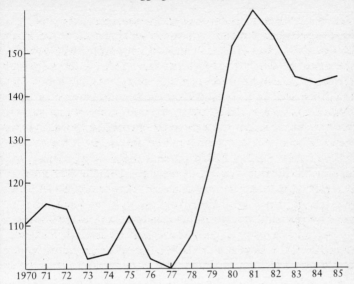

Fig. 20. IMF Index of Relative Unit Normal Labour Costs (1977 = 100), UK 1970–85.

ness (using the overall sterling exchange rate index) fell by no less than 29 per cent. Since 1982 our competitiveness has improved. In 1985 (when the exchange rate index averaged 78), our competitiveness was still 25 per cent lower than it was on average in the 1970s. For even though the pound was not then so expensive in dollars, it was still expensive in the European currencies.

So what explains the movements in the exchange rate? When there is 24-hour trading in currencies in London, New York, and Tokyo, and capital is highly mobile, the exchange rate is basically determined by the mix of monetary and budgetary policy. If monetary policy is relatively tight, with upwards pressure on interest rates, then the exchange rate will tend to appreciate. Tight monetary policy certainly seems to be an important factor explaining the rise of the pound in 1979 and 1980, and still contributes to its high price. But there is of course a rival explanation—North Sea oil.[7] This is how the argument goes. If a country becomes richer through such a discovery, its people will want to consume more of everything, including services. Therefore if there is full employment (and hence limited resources), less manufactures can be produced at home. The extra demand for manufactures will be satisfied from abroad and paid for out of North Sea oil. The demand for British manufactures has to be restrained by a rise in their prices relative to foreign goods. This comes about by an excess demand for British goods, leading to a strong currency and a rise in the price of the pound.

The argument is not watertight. For there are many ways the country could use its new-found wealth. It could decide to invest the extra output rather than consume much more. This investment could either be in new capital equipment produced at home, or it could be in foreign assets bought through a surplus on the balance of payments on current account. In the latter case, there is no reason why the relative prices of British goods should rise, and competitiveness fall. How North Sea oil wealth gets spent is decided by the interaction of private decisions with government policy. The government could certainly have pursued policies that would have limited the rise in the exchange rate. It could have used the oil revenue to buy foreign assets, using pounds to buy foreign currency, thus holding down the price of the pound. Or it could simply have adopted a more expansionary monetary policy, with lower interest rates.

So we have to consider competitiveness as a variable that is within the power of government to control in the short run. There is of course a reason why governments like to be uncompetitive. It means that imports are cheap, which helps to hold down inflation. There may be a case for following this strategy, but, if so, high employment can only be maintained by an expansionary budgetary policy. We discuss these issues in Chapter 12. For the present we are simply concerned with the historical record.

The fact is that about half of the low aggregate demand in the early 1980s *was* due to low competitiveness. Most of the rest was due to the tightness of the budget. Not much seems to be due to world trade being low relative to trend, but this may be due to difficulties of measuring the trend.

BUDGETARY POLICY: US v. EUROPE

Given the importance of budgetary policy in the policy proposals of Part II, it is worth reinforcing here the view that budgets really do matter. As we have seen, unemployment in the US is now roughly back where it was in 1979. In the European Community as a whole it is up 6 percentage points since then, and in Britain up 8 percentage points.

What is the most obvious explanation of these differences? High real interest rates affected both continents, and the US became less competitive relative to Europe. So the much worse unemployment performance in Europe must be mainly due to the difference in budgetary positions. To measure changes in budgetary position we take changes in the actual budget deficit and then eliminate any changes in tax receipts and benefit payments due not to changes in rates but to changes in the level of activity. We also have to replace nominal interest payments by real interest payments. When we have made the adjustments, this is what we find, comparing 1985 with 1979:[8]

	Increase in adjusted budget deficit (% of GDP)	Increase in unemployment
US	+2%	+1%
Britain	−4%	+8%
EEC	−5%	+6%

America has if anything expanded its budget and its unemployment has risen little—the economy has been allowed to function without rude interruption. Britain and Europe have cut their budgets drastically, and higher unemployment has resulted.

This is exactly what the textbooks said would happen. So why was everybody so surprised? They moaned on about 'Eurosclerosis' and there was some truth in the story about rigidities, as we saw in the last chapter. But the fact is that our labour market has not become more rigid in the last six years; quite the contrary. And that is when unemployment nearly trebled. It is only the interaction between rigidities and demand deflation that has caused us problems.[9] So the first step towards understanding the last six years is to understand how tight budgets had their standard textbook effects. This is the story we have told.

ARE REAL WAGES TOO HIGH?

That ends our explanation of the rise in unemployment. The reader may be surprised that we have not discussed the question of whether too high real wages are a cause of unemployment. This is because real wages do not arise spontaneously. They are determined *simultaneously* with unemployment, and do not in some sense precede it. But suppose there is wage push, as illustrated in Figure 13(b). Will higher unemployment be *accompanied* by a higher real wage? Not necessarily. In fact if the price mark-up is independent of unemployment (as in the diagram), unemployment will rise but the real wage will be the same. Thus the problem is not that the real wage is actually too high. It is that at lower unemployment, people would seek too high a real wage target. This is the key. It is real wage *behaviour* which needs to be changed, and not necessarily *real wages*. If incomes policy moderated wage behaviour, it would not necessarily reduce the actual wage.

However, to complete our account we should add a few qualifications. First, if Figure 13(b) is right, wage push would lead to a temporary rise in real wages, though not a permanent increase once unemployment had risen. Second, the feasible real wage curve in Figure 13(b) may well slope up somewhat, with lower price mark-ups at higher unemployment. In this case wage push *would* raise real wages somewhat. Finally, suppose wage push raises the NAIRU. This means that trade balance can be achieved with a less competitive real exchange rate. A real appreciation is therefore likely, leading to a rise in the real wage.[10] We lose in our ability to compete in world markets but our trade balance remains intact. There may be some element of truth in this.

So wage push *may* raise both unemployment and the real wage. But it is still true that the cause of the higher unemployment is not the high real wage but the wage push.

Summary

1. In the long run, unemployment has to settle at the NAIRU, which corresponds to the maximum output which the economy can steadily supply. But in the short run, unemployment is determined by the demand for output.

2. Since 1979 the demand for output has fallen sharply relative to potential output, and is now down by about 7 percentage points. The gap that opened up in 1979–81 has closed very little.

3. The fall in demand has been due mainly to budget cuts and to the rise in the real value of the pound.

4. Since 1979 the share of taxes in national income has risen by over 4 percentage points, while public expenditure (excluding benefits) has barely risen relative to potential output. A similar situation applies to the European Community. By contrast the USA has expanded its budget. Thus the unemployment experience of the two continents is exactly as the elementary textbooks would have predicted from the budgetary changes.

5. The value of the pound rose sharply up to the end of 1981, reducing our ability to compete on world markets. Since then there has been some improvement, but in the year 1985 our competitiveness still averaged 28 per cent less than the average of the 1970s.

6. World real interest rates have risen sharply in the 1980s, discouraging investment in all countries. This hurts us both directly and indirectly (via reduced world trade). But it does not appear to be the main reason why our unemployment has risen.

7. Unemployment is not *caused* by 'too high real wages', but wage push may raise real wages somewhat, as well as raising unemployment.

6

Alternative Theories: Technological Unemployment, Too Many People and Shortage of Capital

We are nearly ready to get on to proposals. But there are still some rival explanations of unemployment that have to be dealt with.

TECHNOLOGICAL UNEMPLOYMENT AND TOO MANY PEOPLE

If you ask the man in the street (*not* Wall Street) what has caused our unemployment, nine times out of ten he will say that it is machines displacing people. In fact for this reason he is often deeply pessimistic about whether we could ever have full employment again.

It is easy to understand his fears. All over the place we see machines taking over people's work. Robots paint our cars, computers maintain our accounts, fork-lift trucks handle our freight. In each work-place where these changes occur, jobs are lost. So it is natural that in a period of rising unemployment, people blame machinery. Exactly the same thing happened in the 1930s. At that time tractors were destroying the jobs of horsemen, mechanical presses were destroying the jobs of welders, and cheap oil was destroying the demand for coal. The same thing happened in the nineteenth century. Threshing machines eliminated jobs in agriculture, and Luddite labourers tried to eliminate threshing machines.

Yet, remarkably, despite constant mechanization ever since the invention of the wheel, there has been no steady upward trend in unemployment (see Fig. 1). New capital constantly destroys jobs, but new jobs spring up elsewhere. How does this happen?

The basic point is that the total level of output is not fixed. When it becomes possible to produce more output, the normal result is that more output is produced. In other words, the level of output adjusts so that the labour market remains in balance. The balance may be unsatisfactory due to the influences discussed in Chapter 4 (social security, unions, and the like). But in the long term the balance is not adversely affected by productivity growth.

To see this, let us look at the historical record. This shows clearly that, in the long term, output goes up if output per worker rises or if the labour force increases. Figure 21 graphs output per worker, and Figure 22 graphs the labour force. In Figure 23 we put these two together to get a measure of full-employment output:

Full-employment output = Labour force × Output per worker.

Figure 23 also shows actual output. If people wished to argue that output does not in the long run mainly react to full-employment output, they would find it hard to produce any alternative explanation of output that was remotely as plausible. However in the short term there are divergences which can last for decades. We are currently in such a divergence, and we were in the 1930s. In the figure, the gap between potential and actual output is scaled to measure the 'output gap' as a proportion of potential output. This is high now and was high in the 1930s.

The same point is made in Figure 22, which shows the relation of employment to the labour force (and therefore abstracts from the issue of productivity growth). Again if people wished to argue that employment does not in the long run respond to the size of the labour force, they would be hard pressed to find any alternative explanation of the long-term movement of employment that was remotely as plausible. When one considers the matter, it is really quite remarkable that the number of jobs should bear any relation to the number of people wanting work. There must be some equilibrating mechanism at work. People who doubt this should be challenged to produce some other

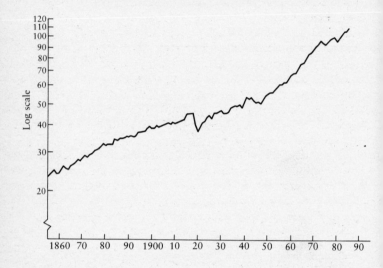

Fig. 21. GDP per Worker, 1855–1985 (index with 1979 = 100)

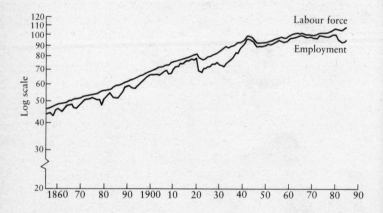

Fig. 22. Labour Force and Employment, 1855–1985 (index with employment in 1979 = 100).

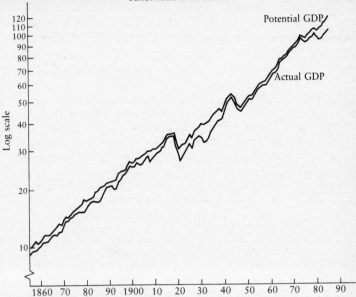

Fig. 23. Actual and 'Potential' Gross Domestic Product, 1855–1985 (index with actual GDP in 1979 = 100)

explanation of the astonishing facts shown in Figure 22. Whether we look at our country over time or at a cross-section of countries (as in Fig. 9 for Europe, the US, and Japan) one is struck by the long-term effect of labour force growth upon employment.

It is all very well to say that an equilibrating mechanism exists. But what is it? In Chapter 3 we described the basic mechanism by which, so long as inflation was not rushing up or down, the economy would settle at a level of unemployment determined by the various supply-side factors discussed in Chapters 3 and 4. In the short run, as we explained, output can be driven away from its long-run level by 'overkill'. In this case output will be too low. But the answer then is more demand.

The one fatal heresy in economic analysis is to take output as given. That is the 'lump of output' fallacy. You must always have a theory of how output is determined and you must never say, 'Higher output per worker reduces employment, because it reduces the employment needed to produce a given output'. Likewise you must never say 'More people cause unemployment', unless you can explain why output will not grow.

STRUCTURAL ASPECTS OF THE IMPACT OF TECHNOLOGY

Having said this, there are still some very important issues about technology and employment. We have seen that any long-run impact can only come about through the mechanisms discussed in Chapters 3 and 4. One problem could be greater mismatch.

How far does new machinery and new technology alter the pattern of demand for labour and thus tend to increase mismatch? There are two kinds of new technology: product innovations, which produce new goods, and process innovations, which involve new ways of producing old goods. Product innovation may be less of a problem since it must create new jobs. But it can generate major shortages of labour if the new jobs are in high employment areas rather than where jobs are being lost in the older industries.

Process innovation is what people mainly fear—new ways of producing old goods. Yet in fact when an industry becomes more automated, employment in it can go up or down.

It depends first on how output changes. This in turn depends on how much the relative product price falls when production costs are reduced, and how far output expands when the relative price falls. Consider for example office automation. The computer and the word-processor have enormously reduced the labour needed to produce a given amount of typed information. But office employment has not fallen. For, since typed information has become cheaper, people have decided they want much more of it. In general one would expect industries facing foreign competition to be the most price-sensitive. Innovation there would be particularly favourable to employment, though often it will only stave off the job losses which would otherwise have happened due to falls in competitors' prices caused by innovation abroad. But the first issue is always the size of the positive effect on output.

The second issue is the size of the negative effect on the number of jobs per unit of output. It is quite possible for these two effects to cancel out. In general it is clear that jobs are more likely to increase the more price-sensitive the demand for output and the less 'labour-saving' the innovation. Thus there are cases where the balance of effects is positive (computers), and where it is negative (agriculture). The greater the change in either direction, the greater the dislocation. And clearly the dislocation will be greater, the more technical change is going on.

This brings us to the key factual question: How rapid has technical change been recently? As Figure 21 showed, the average rate of productivity growth from 1973 to date has been lower than in the thirty years that preceded it. So we simply cannot blame higher unemployment on higher productivity growth—it was not higher. In fact, unemployment was much lower in the 1960s when productivity growth was higher. So let that be an end to the myth of rising technological unemployment.

There is one other important issue in relation to technical progress: How does it affect the equilibrium real wage? Fears have often been expressed that, if technical progress is sufficiently labour-saving, it could reduce the equilibrium real wage. This would make it difficult, initially at least, to maintain industrial peace. The work which Nickell and I have done suggests that technical progress has in the last 25 years had a fairly neutral effect on the real wage.[1] But real wages have grown sharply due to capital accumulation. Since technical progress rarely happens without capital accumulation, there is no obvious problem from this quarter.

FOREIGN COMPETITION

Another issue which bothers many people is the feeling that we are steadily and inexorably losing our ability to compete in the world. The newly industrializing countries (NICs) can undercut us on low tech because their wages are low, and the US can dominate us in high tech. So, many people feel, What is left?

The answer is, A great deal. For the last six years the British trade balance has generally been favourable. This is partly due to oil. But there is plenty else that we are exporting, especially chemicals and machinery of all kinds. Apart from the problem of real wages discussed at the end of the last chapter, advanced economies constantly adapt to changing world trade patterns and find a niche for themselves, so that their trade balance becomes roughly in balance. The fact that we are importing consumer goods like mad from the NICs is the mirror image of the fact that they are importing machinery like mad from us. In fact our trade balance with them is in our favour.

Clearly, new patterns of foreign competition lead to structural shifts in labour demand which tend to increase the mismatch between vacancies and unemployment. But shifts in foreign competition have been going on since the industrial revolution, and in Chapter 4 we found no evidence of growing mismatch in the labour force in recent years.

SHORTAGE OF CAPITAL

So far we have disposed of three myths relating to the *long-term* trend of unemployment: it is not up because of more rapid technological change, nor because of too many people, nor because of foreign competition. We turn now to a more short-run issue. This is the notion that today unemployment has to be high because there is no capital around to employ the whole labour force.

There can certainly be occasions when this is a problem, as in post-war bomb-shattered Germany. Is it the case today? The best evidence on this comes from the answers which the Confederation of British Industries get in their Survey of Industrial Trends. They ask their members in manufacturing industry 'Is your output over the next four months likely to be limited by shortage of capacity?' The answers are shown in Figure 24, panel (a). The figures certainly do not suggest a major capacity crunch. The CBI also ask 'Are you now working below capa-

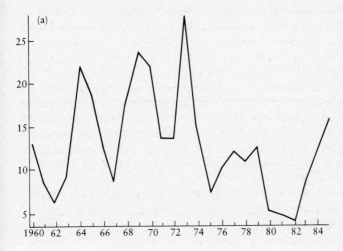

Fig. 24(a). Percentage of Firms Reporting Output to be Constrained by Shortage of Physical Capacity (1960–85)

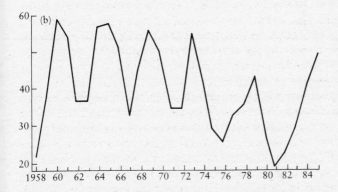

Fig. 24(b). Percentage of Firms Not Reporting Below-Capacity Working (1958–85).

city?' The answers here are reported in panel (b) and suggest a tighter situation, with capacity utilization a bit closer to its 1979 level but nowhere near to earlier peaks. In any case all agree capacity utilization is nearer to its historic average than labour utilization—as measured in Figure 16 by vacancies or by shortages of skilled labour.

So should we worry? There are many reasons not to do so. First, the fear of inflationary pressure connected with high capacity utilization stems from the past correlation between the two. But if labour market bottlenecks now are less, the correlation may change. In considering inflation we should mainly worry about the labour market and commodity prices, rather than the market for output.

Second, the notion of capacity is not in any sense absolute. Many different numbers of workers can be usefully employed at any instant with a given set of machines. In a given office block or a restaurant, the number of workers present can be raised even more. How many are profitable is a matter of costs and returns. On top of this, extra shifts can be worked. Most capital is worked only on one shift, with only 14 per cent of all worker-hours in manufacturing being worked outside 8 a.m. to 6 p.m.[2]

Finally, the amount of capital can itself be altered quite quickly if there is a need for it. In the recession there has been a massive scrapping of capital due to low expected demand. If this were reversed, capital could be quite quickly built up. That is the message that comes from most analyses of investment behaviour. Getting the new capital is generally not too difficult, since 39 per cent of capital equipment is imported and we are therefore quite small in the market.

The 'supply-side pessimists' maintain that this fails to take into account the problem of excessive real wages. But, as we have argued, too high real wages are not the fundamental problem, since real wages are mainly determined by the collective behaviour of employers. The problem is mainly *not* that real wages are too high but that workers *aspire to* too high real wages. This is the fundamental explanation we have given for the current high NAIRU, with overkill as an additional factor making for high unemployment. It is against that background that we now turn to possible remedies.

Summary

1. High productivity growth is not the reason why unemployment has risen. Productivity growth has been much lower in the last decade than in the 1960s. Yet unemployment was lower in the 1960s.

2. Labour force growth is not the reason why unemployment has risen. In most periods the demand for output grows in line with the growth of the labour force and the growth rate of productivity. In recent years this has not been allowed to happen, and today's unemployment is directly due to low output demand.

3. Shortage of capital is not a major obstacle to increases in employment. Most new jobs will come in services, where the link between capital and employment is less clear than in manufacturing. In manufacturing, capital can be worked more intensively, or, given a good prospect for future demand, new capital can be acquired, if necessary from abroad. The main source of inflationary pressure is in the labour market rather than the product market.

PART 2
THE WAY FORWARD

7

Cutting Unemployment Using Both Blades of the Scissors: More Demand and Improved Supply

As we have seen, unemployment is determined in the medium term by supply factors and in the short term by demand. To reduce it we must increase demand. But this will soon lead to bottlenecks unless at the same time we do something about the supply side. Operating on demand without supply, *or* vice versa, will be of limited use. But if we use both blades of the scissors, we can make a real cut. We want to get away from the one-armed bandits who think in terms of only supply or only demand. It is always better to be ambidextrous.

Because of the NAIRU there is a long-term limit to the output which the economy can supply. The purpose of supply-side policies is to reduce the NAIRU. But this should not be done independently of demand, for two reasons. First, the pattern of demand itself influences the NAIRU. If demand is targeted more effectively at the high unemployment groups, then total unemployment can be lower without inflation increasing. Second, if the NAIRU is reduced and spending is not increased, employment will not rise initially. Instead inflation will come down further. This will in due course improve our competitiveness and thus create more jobs (provided monetary targets are not adjusted down in line with inflation, thus inducing an appreciation of the nominal exchange rate). But the process will take time, and there is no reason why we should wait that long.

With our present critical levels of unemployment, we should provide the extra demand straight away, up to the level of our supply capacity. Inflation is not so evil that we should now give priority to reducing it further, rather than to reducing unemployment as quickly as possible. The government gives the impression that it has a different view and is only willing to let the economy be reflated through lower inflation, rather than through higher spending at existing levels of inflation.[1] This is a disastrous error.

CRITERIA FOR A PACKAGE THAT IS SUPPLY-SIDE FRIENDLY

We need a major programme to increase spending in a way that is consistent with non-increasing inflation. It must therefore have five main features.

(i) *The additional demand must be 'targeted' at the high-unemployment groups*

- the long-term unemployed,
- semi- and unskilled workers,
- workers in high unemployment regions,
- construction workers,
- young workers.

It is no good spreading money across the board and just bidding up the wages of groups that are already fully employed.

(ii) *The increase in the budget deficit for each additional job should be as small as possible*, so as not to alarm the financial markets. This again means concentrating on measures that will employ low-wage workers and in addition avoiding import-intensive activities.

The 'budget deficit cost per job' differs enormously between different programmes. For example, the net budgetary cost per job on the Community Programme (discussed later) is around £2,000 p.a., while the net budgetary cost per job created by income tax cuts is, say, £40,000 p.a.[2] This is because so much of the additional expenditure caused by tax cuts goes on imports or on goods produced by high-wage labour.

It is obviously true that the *output per job* is less for a job on the Community Programme than for a job created by tax cuts. But it does not seem likely that the output difference could possibly be as much as in the ratio 2:40. So £40,000 spent on the

Community Programme rather than tax cuts would not only generate 20 times more jobs but also more output. Since the efficiency of the economy is measured by its total output, the Community Programme does all right on that score, and does extremely well on the score of jobs.

This has a major influence on our strategy. Suppose we run programmes costing twice as much as the Community Programme. We could still provide $\frac{3}{4}$ million more jobs that way at a cost to the Exchequer of £3 billion (or 1 per cent of national income). Providing the same number of jobs by general tax cuts would cost £30 billion (or 10 per cent of national income). The latter would create a major financial panic.

Thus our two basic criteria are that jobs should be targeted towards underemployed groups (to avoid wage pressure), and that the budgetary cost per job should be as low as possible, subject to the workers producing a reasonable level of useful output. But there are three further criteria.

(iii) *We must take steps to improve the supply of labour*, so that it is better matched to demand.

(iv) *We should promote the private sector* (other things equal) rather than the public services. The collapse of employment which we have experienced has been almost entirely in the private sector (and the public corporations).[3] So, other things being equal, we are more interested in stimulating private than public employment. There should be some increase in the Health Service, but such detail is not central to the basic thought of this book—how to get non-inflationary growth. This requires a fifth principle.

(v) *The whole package must be backed by a firm and viable incomes policy.*

THE PACKAGE PROPOSED

A sensible package based on these principles would have five main items

1. A new deal for the long-term unemployed.

2. Restructuring employers' National Insurance Contributions in favour of the unskilled and the regions.
3. More investment on the infrastructure, involving the construction industry.
4. A new incentive to employers to train their workers.
5. A tax-based incomes policy.

These represent explicit attempts to deal with the main supply-side problems discussed in Chapter 4, which were:

- long-duration unemployment linked to open-ended benefits with no effective manpower policy (tackled by item 1)
- mismatch (tackled by items 2–4)
- union power (tackled by item 5)

The next three chapters describe our package in detail, taking the policies in that order. First, we propose a new deal for the long-term unemployed, then we show how extra spending can ease the mismatch in the labour force, and finally we outline our incomes policy.

AGGREGATE DEMAND, INTEREST RATES AND THE EXCHANGE RATE

Our strategy is to expand the demand for output in a way that also increases the ability of the economy to supply output without extra inflation. The key to reducing unemployment is producing more output. An annual growth rate of at least 2 per cent would be needed to hold unemployment constant. To close the output gap, we need growth rates of at least 4 per cent for some years. Such growth rates have been achieved before, when there was gross slack in the economy. Between 1933 and 1937, for example, the economy grew at an average of $4\frac{1}{2}$ per cent a year.

To achieve higher output growth there has to be higher demand for output. Some of this demand will come from the government through government purchases, but much of it will have to come from private sector demand, encouraged through lower taxes on employment or extra subsidies.

These policies will inevitably cost the government money. It will be spending more and taxing at lower rates. So its deficit will have to rise by at least 1 per cent of national income a year for at least two years (i.e. by at least 2 per cent after two years). As the economy regains its momentum, the injection could then be reduced. But without a big priming of the pump, the economy will never get back to firing on all four cylinders, and there will be no hope of reducing unemployment below 2 million.

If the deficit is going to rise that much, this raises the obvious question of whether such a policy is not self-defeating. Might it not lead to extra inflation, so that the extra spending never translates into higher output? Or might not interest rates go so high as to cut back investment by as much as other real spending increases, leaving the number of jobs unchanged?

To answer the question about inflation, we should remember that prices depend essentially on wages and the prices of imports. We have already taken enormous pains to avoid any extra wage inflation. How to control import prices? These depend essentially on the level of the exchange rate. If the value of the pound falls, import prices rise. Thus a key element in policy during the recovery phase must be to hold the level of the exchange rate steady. This in turn means that real interest rates cannot be cut relative to real interest rates abroad, otherwise people will not want to hold their wealth in pounds. Looser monetary policy (defined as cuts in *relative* real interest rates) is thus not an option.

The decision that we cannot afford a major fall in the exchange rate means that we cannot rely on improved competitiveness as a way of getting more jobs. That is why the budget is so important. It is the only safe method of injecting more demand into the economy.[4]

But the question then arises of what happens to interest rates. If the public debt goes up, will not people insist on higher interest rates as the price for lending the extra money? It is not that obvious. For we now have a highly integrated world capital market. If our interest rates rise ever so little relatively to those in New York or Tokyo, one might expect a lot of money to come flooding our way. But even if our interest rates needed to rise somewhat, this need not be a disaster. It hasn't been for the US economy and so would not be for ours, especially if we spent some money on temporary (time-limited) investment incentives. The factors affecting interest rates are complex and are therefore the main topic of Chapter 11, which sets our proposals in their full 'macro-economic' context.

There is one other 'macro-economic' issue—the trade balance. If we expand our output but do not improve our competitiveness, our trade balance will deteriorate. This would not of course happen if other countries expanded at the same time as we did. This is the argument for a 'concerted reflation'. We should all press for it, but we cannot rely on it. Thus at some point later we may need to improve our competitiveness by a depreciation. This would be the main consideration that might require us to raise our relative interest rates now (to compensate holders of sterling for the expected depreciation). We cannot therefore pretend that interest rates might not be affected by our policy. But, if they rose somewhat, it is inconceivable that this could anywhere near offset the job-creating impact of our policy. The US has pursued a policy along the lines we are advocating. It held its interest rates so high that until 1985 the dollar steadily appreciated in a quite unnecessary way. But this did not abort the powerful effects of expansionary budgets on spending and thus on jobs. Since these are major issues, we shall return to them in detail in Chapter 11.

That will end our case. However there are pessimists who believe there is no way in which the total work available can be increased, because of capital shortage, satiation, or whatever. For them the only way forward is to share the work around as many people as possible, and to encourage the old to retire. We have already argued against the premises of this argument (in Chapter 6). In Chapter 12 we show that the prescription would not work.

We are now ready to examine our package in detail.

Summary

1. This chapter outlines the structure of the second half of the book.

2. The aim of our policies is to increase demand in a way that does not increase inflation.

3. Wage inflation can be contained if extra demand is targeted to unemployed workers or those in general excess supply. An incomes policy is also essential.

4. Import price inflation can be controlled by holding the exchange rate at around its present level. This may require somewhat higher interest rates relative to world levels, but there is no danger that this could be a major offset to our programme of generating jobs.

5. To reduce unemployment below 2 million, output will need to grow by at least 4 per cent a year for some years, as it did from 1933 to 1937.

6. The budget deficit will need to grow by at least 1 per cent of national income per annum for at least two years (so that it would then be higher by at least 2 per cent of national income). As the economy moved into self-sustaining growth, this injection could then be withdrawn.

8

A New Deal for the Long-Term Unemployed

In thinking about unemployment it is essential to think big. It is no good nibbling away at the problem, on the grounds that this is the best we can hope for. We must have a vision which offers hope of reducing unemployment to the levels of the late 1970s. The next three chapters are an attempt to provide such a vision.

The most scandalous feature of our present situation is long-term unemployment (meaning unemployment lasting more than a year). There are now $1\frac{1}{3}$ million people in this position—40 per cent of all the unemployed. There are no extenuating circumstances for this. Most of these people are not near retirement—only 15 per cent are over 55. The majority are in the prime of their lives, people who would be the backbone of a properly functioning economy. Half a million have been unemployed for over three years.

Such unemployment is wasteful and costly. It is deeply demoralizing for the great majority of the unemployed, who lose their skills and their work habits, and it costs the rest of us a great deal of money spent on social security.

THE CASE FOR TARGETING

There are very few benefits to be set against these costs. Unemployment as a whole helps to restrain inflation, but, as we have said, research on wage behaviour makes it clear that the long-term unemployed account for little or none of this effect. It is only those who have recently lost their jobs and who are actively looking for work who exert some pressure to keep wages down. The long-term unemployed have largely given up hope.

This helps explain why, despite the high levels of unemployment now prevailing in Britain (and Europe generally) inflation is falling so slowly. For, as Figure 4 shows, in the last five years the number of people unemployed for less than a year has actually fallen somewhat; the total increase in unemployment is accounted for by those unemployed for more than a year. Thus re-employing the long-term unemployed would do little to rekindle inflation. Such re-employment must therefore be a priority for the Government. For long-term unemployment, which represents the greatest unnecessary waste of resources in our society, is also a problem on which the Government can have a major impact at no enormous cost to itself.

The long-term unemployed are currently costing us a fortune. On average they receive nearly £50 a week in benefit. And they pay much less in taxes than if they were employed. On average a person who 'becomes' long-term unemployed by embarking on his 13th month of unemployment can expect to remain unemployed for another year. So it would pay the rest of us to spend at least £40 a week for one year to get the person employed (assuming that no other workers were displaced into unemployment). And this ignores altogether the benefit to the unemployed person from getting back to work.

Unfortunately, as we shall see, it is wishful thinking to suppose that we can get people back to work at no net cost to the budget. But we can certainly get the long-term unemployed back to work at a relatively low cost. Since there is work crying out to be done, let us marry the workers to the work.

There is thus an overwhelming case for moving to a position where every long-term unemployed person is guaranteed the offer of a job lasting at least one year. This is the policy of all the opposition parties in Britain and has recently been supported by the all-party House of Commons Employment Committee (1986). The question has always been how it could be achieved.

There are two standard methods of targeted job creation: one is public employment, and the other is job subsidies to the private sector. Given the scale of the problem, we have to use both. In fact, if we are to achieve our goal, it is best to bring them together in a single programme operated by the Manpower Services Commission. This puts the responsibility of achieving the guarantee clearly in one place, as it was with the successfully operated guarantee of a training place for all 16-year olds (the Youth Training Scheme). It ensures that any private sector subsidies receive full publicity, and sponsors are solicited. But it must not lead to wasteful and pointless make-work schemes in the public sector. The whole justification of the policy is that it increases national output, as well as providing jobs. It thus passes the test of social efficiency as well as fairness.

Let us first outline the strategy, then lay out its rationale, and then describe in more detail the nuts and bolts, for those who are interested.

THE STRATEGY[1]

Decide now to provide a million extra jobs to be filled by the long-term unemployed (LTU). Since the Community Programme will be providing nearly $\frac{1}{4}$ million jobs, we need to find another $\frac{3}{4}$ million. These jobs would be in three fields:

(i) a building improvement programme, with public and private projects, but managed mainly by private contractors,

(ii) extra private sector jobs outside construction, generated by suitable financial inducements,

(iii) more posts in personal social services (especially community care) and in the National Health Service.

The plan would build up over three years, at the end of which every LTU would be guaranteed the offer of a one-year place on one of these programmes. A commitment would be made now to deliver this guarantee within three years.

The whole plan would be run by the Manpower Services Commission. In each area there would be a team led jointly by a spending officer and the head of the Employment Service. It would be their job to reduce long-term unemployment to the greatest possible degree.

During the build-up, the plan would raise public borrowing by about £1 billion each year (i.e. by the third year, borrowing would be just over £3 billion higher than otherwise). Let me now explain the reasoning behind this approach.

CRITERIA

There seem to be five basic criteria required for a sensible policy.

1. Any new job created for the long-term unemployed should be *additional* to those that would otherwise exist. This is for two reasons. First, existing workers and their unions must not feel that the scheme reduces existing employment opportunities for other types of workers. Second, the economic aim of the exercise is to expand employment.

2. Employment should be expanded at the *lowest feasible net cost per job* to the Exchequer. This criterion must however be tempered by considering the value of the output produced. More generally, we could choose projects on the basis of the cost for a given increase in social welfare.

We have already seen that the Community Programme scores well on this basis. So one approach would be to expand the Community Programme. At present the programme is geared towards providing 255,000 places. Sponsors approach the Manpower Services Commission with projects (largely in the area of environmental improvement or social services). Sponsors are local authorities or voluntary organizations. Projects must be work that would not otherwise be done for at least two years and must not yield private profit. Projects generally require the support of the Manpower Services Commission's Area Manpower Board, which consists of union and employer representatives plus independent members. If approved, the projects are then funded by the Manpower Services Commission and manned by long-term unemployed people employed for one year. Pay is limited to an average of £67 a week. Workers receive the hourly rate for the job, and given the low weekly pay, hours often average around 30 a week, rather than full time.

There are at least two problems with expanding the scheme further. First, it would be difficult to find large numbers of additional projects that are of adequate social value, unless some private profit is allowed. Second, jobs on the Community Programme are project-based, and often involve no contact with a regular employer. The fact that they are temporary does not mean that the money spent does not create employment, while the money spent on tax cuts does; for employment created by either method only continues so long as the extra spending continues. But jobs which are both temporary and unconnected with a regular employer are not so satisfactory for the individual. They do not encourage training and can lead to a waste of whatever training is given. These two points lead to our next two criteria.

3. The work done should be as far as possible the work of *highest social value* that is not currently being done. This criterion can only be partially satisfied, given that all projects must be additional and seen to be so. But, if we are going to have a major expansion of employment, we do have to make sure that what is produced is really useful. This must mean using the private sector as well as the public sector.

4. Unemployed people should as far as possible be taken into *regular jobs* with regular employers. In general, workers perform best and receive the most relevant training if they are employed on standard employment contracts. This means exploiting the widest possible opportunities, again including the private sector as well as the public sector.

5. Workers should receive the rate for the job and be able to work a *full week*.

THE SCALE OF THE PROBLEM

Turning to the number of extra jobs needed, there are now 1.6 million long-term unemployed (if, like the government, we include the under 25s who have been out of work for over six months). To guarantee each of them the offer of a place, how many jobs should we need to create? It is difficult to be sure, but a target of 1 million places seems sufficient since not all would wish the kind of jobs on offer. Thus we need to be able to offer a stock of approximately 1 million extra jobs—on top of the number of jobs that would otherwise exist in the economy.

Some might argue that this is not enough, on the grounds that we also have to provide for the new flow into long-term unemployment. But this is a confusion. At present the flow out of long-term unemployment into work is the same as the flow into long-term unemployment—1 million per year.[2] So the flow is being catered for. Our task is to provide ways of reducing the stock. One million jobs should probably suffice to deliver the guarantee.

Places on this scale would only be needed for a few years, while the stock was being reduced. Thus we have to envisage a three-year build-up to a stock of 1 million places, followed after a few years by an equivalent build-down.

The question then arises of where the extra jobs should be found. One obvious area is in urban rehabilitation, since the high unemployment areas are also the most physically derelict in Britain. (In high unemployment areas the proportion of unemployed who have been out of work for over a year tends to be higher than the national average.[3])

But there is clearly a limit to the number who can be employed in urban rehabilitation. The construction industry is currently employing (as employees and self-employed) about $\frac{1}{2}$ million fewer workers than in 1974, and 200,000 less than in 1979. Given the appalling backlog in maintenance work that has developed over the last five years, it seems reasonable to imagine an additional employment of say 300,000 long-term unemployed workers for a limited period during which much of this backlog is cleared.

Another fruitful area for extra work is social services and health. But here again there is a limit (discussed below). This means that we have to include the private sector outside construction. We should not try to allocate funds centrally between the different industries, but it is useful to have a broad picture of where the existing jobs are, as shown in Table 9.

One should note in particular the obvious scope for expanding employment of less-skilled people in distribution, hotels, catering, and repairs, and also in cleaning.

The aim is therefore to produce $\frac{3}{4}$ million additional jobs on top of the planned $\frac{1}{4}$ million on the Community Programme, giving ourselves three years to achieve the build-up. The pro-

Table 9. Number of Employees June 1985, by industry (excluding Armed Forces) (millions)

Agriculture	0.3	
Energy and water supply	0.6	
Manufacturing	5.4	
Construction	0.9	(0.10 in local authorities) (there are also 0.5 million self-employed)
Distribution, hotels, catering, repairs	4.4	
Transport and communication	1.3	
Banking, finance, and insurance	1.9	
Public administration and defence	1.5	
Education	1.6	
Health	1.3	
Social services	0.5	(0.3 in local authorities)
Other services	1.1	
	20.7	

posal for finding the ¾ million places would be as shown in Table 10.

The costings are approximate. The net cost to public borrowing when the scheme has fully built up would be just over £3 billion, supporting 0.75 million jobs. The gross cost would be £4.8 billion (£3.3 billion plus about £2,000 per person unemployment benefits saved). If one thinks of the build-up of these totals over three years, we have an addition to public borrowing of only about £1 billion a year, which is small relative to many other possible changes.

Table 10. How to Create the Additional Jobs

	Net additional jobs (million)	Net cost per job (£)	Total net cost (£ billion)
Building Improvement Programme	0.30	5,000	1.5
Private sector scheme	0.35	4,000	1.4
Social services and health	0.10	4,000	0.4
	0.75		3.3

The whole programme should be administered by the Manpower Services Commission. In each area there would be a long-term unemployment working group led by two senior officials: one spending officer plus the head of the Employment Service. The latter would know that his performance would be judged in part by the placement of long-term unemployed in his region. The other senior officer would be responsible for the spending of a specific budget for the long-term unemployed, based broadly on the number of LTUs in the region. He could spend it on any of the three schemes, which we now look at in detail.

BUILDING IMPROVEMENT PROGRAMME

Much of the fabric of our cities is in terrible disrepair. The NEDO report on the infrastructure has shown the size of the problem in housing, schools, hospitals, and roads.[4] In many areas expenditure today could save much larger expenditure tomorrow. Much of the work to be done requires relatively little skill, and many of the unemployed do in any case have substantial skills, either as construction workers or from DIY. When there is so much work to be done and so many who would be glad to do it, it makes obvious sense to bring them together.

In construction it is extremely difficult to secure 'additionality' (i.e. that the jobs paid for are additional to existing jobs) by giving money directly to employers and insisting they employ extra workers. The reason is that employment in each firm varies so much, as projects come and go. Thus in construction, additionality has to be secured by regulating the pattern of spending. The Manpower Services Commission therefore decides on the projects to be supported. However, efficiency requires that private contractors be normally employed to manage the projects and to supply any additional skilled labour required. They could therefore tender for projects, on the basis of a management fee. Thus no employer could complain that he lacked an opportunity to compete for the work. Direct labour organizations could also put in tenders. The long-term unemployed would be paid the rate for the job, with a maximum average wage cost laid down by the Manpower Services Commission (see below).

First we need to look closer at the projects. The obvious kinds of work are on the external and internal decoration and renovation of houses, schools and hospitals, minor road repairs, and site clearance and environmental improvement. The work on housing would include private houses, especially those belonging to pensioners and others on low incomes. Council houses could be included, where it was clear that they would not otherwise be dealt with. Privately rented houses could be included, provided the tenants were low-paid and the landlord paid a reasonable fee. Other work could also be considered if additionality could be established. Local authorities and NHS would probably not pay for work done for them, to avoid political difficulties about additionality.

The problem of additionality always arises, but it is important to be clear about the general economic issue. If by misadventure one of our schemes leads a council to do less of its own work and cut its rates, this does not mean that no new jobs have been created. For the cut in rates will generate spending which employs people who could not otherwise be employed. Similarly, if a private person is deterred from a particular item of spending by an LTU scheme, he is likely to spend money on something else. Thus at the worst the schemes provide as many jobs as tax cuts, but even then they are better than tax cuts because they provide the jobs for the right people. However, if the additionality criterion is achieved, more jobs can be created for a given sum of money. And, very importantly, no individual will feel aggrieved because he has lost his job in order that someone else can gain one. It is therefore important to aim hard at additionality, even though we know it will not always be achieved.

Workers need to be paid enough to make it worth their while working. The Community Programme places a limit of £67 a week on the average pay per person. Workers are paid the hourly rate for the job and often work less than a full week. Such an arrangement is unsatisfactory, and explains why the Community Programme attracts few family men. A more sensible maximum average weekly pay would be say £105, with workers paid the hourly rate for the job. This should make it possible to provide full-time jobs for those who wanted them.

The cost per job would be more than on the Community Programme for a number of reasons. There is the higher cost of management and supervision; there is the higher cost of materials, due to the more ambitious nature of the work; and there are higher wages. After allowing for savings on unemployment benefits, the net cost per job should be around £5,000 (compared with £2,000 on the Community Programme). This does not allow for any receipts for services rendered. If these were significant, the cost would come down to nearer £4,000.

The scheme outlined above is essentially the same in structure as the recent CBI proposals for a Building Improvement Programme.[5]

THE PRIVATE SECTOR OUTSIDE CONSTRUCTION

We cannot deal with a problem of the size we face without increasing the private employment of LTUs—in as many sectors as possible. Therefore, outside construction, private employers taking on LTUs could be paid £40 a week for the first year of their employment, provided that non-subsidized employment did not fall. (This could be monitored through National Insurance records). Provided the scheme were effectively promoted by the Manpower Services Commission, it could create about 0.35 million new jobs, by making it more worthwhile for firms to employ labour.[6]

Private employers wishing to use the scheme would approach the Manpower Services Commission, and the Manpower Services Commission would also be actively trying to place workers.

A reason for suggesting £40 is that this is a bit less than the average benefit an LTU receives. Moreover, as we have seen, an LTU can currently expect to remain unemployed for at least a further year.[7] Thus, if we employ the person for a year at a cost of about £2,000 (52×40), we also save at least £2,000 in benefit.

However there is of course the problem of deadweight cost: some of those subsidized would have been employed anyway. But we can easily calculate the maximum deadweight cost. This corresponds to the whole existing flow out of LTU into the private sector. This is about 0.5 million a year,[8] making a deadweight cost of £1.0 billion. On this basis the net cost per job would be about £3,000 per annum, but since we want to be sure not to underestimate the cost, let us assume a net cost per job of £4,000 per annum.

What we are proposing is a kind of marginal employment subsidy—that is, a subsidy linked to increases in total employment. This kind of subsidy is inherently more effective than an across-the-board subsidy, or indeed the general cut in employers' National Insurance contributions so often advocated by the Confederation of British Industry. For suppose the government cuts employers' National Insurance contributions by 2 per cent. Most of this will reduce the cost of labour which firms would employ anyway. It is nearly all 'deadweight'. But we could instead use the money to provide a real incentive to take on more labour. We could offer a subsidy of, say, 50 per cent for all new jobs created. This would probably cost the same as the 2 per cent across the board, assuming it were paid out for 4 per cent of the labour force (including deadweight). Clearly the marginal employment subsidy is the more effective way of using the money since it cuts the cost of extra labour by 50 per cent rather than 2 per cent.

There is always uncertainty about the size of the deadweight cost of any marginal employment subsidy to all kinds of labour. However if we limit the subsidy to long-term unemployed people, we can at once calculate the maximum deadweight. The calculations are given above. This is a further argument for highly targeted subsidies.

Clearly the subsidy will lead to some hiring of long-term unemployed people in preference to short-term unemployed, and not only to additional hirings. However, in order to control inflation, a rotation of this kind has definite advantages. A further problem might be that workers could actually look less hard for work in months 9–12 of their unemployment, because they knew they could get a job at 12 months. Clearly such distortions will occur, but they could not possibly be big enough to outweigh the advantages of the scheme.

SOCIAL SERVICES AND HEALTH

Finally, there are obvious unmet needs in personal social services and health. The current move to community care requires at least 50,000 more workers in the community, while the National Health Service is short of orderlies, cleaners, laundry, and catering staff. Present resources are a constraint. The solution is not just to provide more money, but to provide more money linked to spending it on the long-term unemployed—say 50,000 people in social services (e.g. working in short-stay units or providing support for those discharged from hospital), and 50,000 in the National Health Service.

It would be very inefficient not to embed the additional workers in the regular occupational structure, as that would lead to inefficient working—and an interrupted relationship with clients. The Community Programme has been much criticized on these grounds.

When the year was up, the worker would cease to be subsidized. But he would not necessarily change jobs, and one would hope that many workers could be kept on on an unsubsidized basis, given the relatively high turnover in these occupations. The MSC would naturally hope that the employer would at that point take on another subsidized worker.

Given the occupations we have in mind, the net cost would be about £80 a week, with a gross cost of £120 (equal to the average wage, averaged over community-care work and less-skilled work in the National Health Service).

THE PHILOSOPHY OF SPECIAL MEASURES

Some people have reservations about special measures as a way of cutting unemployment. They ask: If we are going to spend more, why not spend it through normal channels? The answer is that such expenditure would be far more likely to lead to the bidding up of wages. Much of it would thus be dissipated in extra inflation rather than extra jobs. That is the first reason why we want to concentrate expenditure directly on those who have been out of work for a long time. The second reason is that it is a relatively cheap way of creating jobs, and the third is the obvious moral case for helping those who are most in trouble.

What is proposed is not 'make-work'. It is real work, producing socially useful output. In the social services, National Health Service and the non-construction private sector, these jobs would be regular jobs, although government financial support would end after a year.[9] In the building improvement programme the jobs would be explicitly temporary (one year), and it would be important that those involved received intensive counselling and placement as the year comes to an end. A key part of the strategy is the obligation on the Manpower Services Commission to give priority to the placement of the long-term unemployed (and of the ex-long-term unemployed after their one-year placements.)

The whole aim of the programme is that ultimately the participants get permanent jobs. We cannot guarantee someone a permanent job. But by giving him work experience for at least a year, we can restore his morale and improve his skills.

Long-term unemployment on the present scale requires the kind of response which the nation gave in wartime. The expenditure involved is not unmanageable and the problem *can* be solved.

BENEFITS FOR THE LONG-TERM UNEMPLOYED

As we have said, our aim is to eliminate long-term unemployment. We are offering everyone a job after a year of being unemployed. This raises the obvious question: Should someone who could have a job be entitled to benefit if he chooses not to take it?

Under existing law he could be refused benefit (though an administrative decision has been made that people who refuse a place on the Community Programme still get benefit). In Sweden, which has in many ways a more generous welfare state than Britain, those who refuse a place on a public programme are refused benefit. By the time they have been unemployed for a year all unemployed Swedes will have been offered a job or a place on a training scheme. If they refuse it, they no longer qualify for benefits. In any case Unemployment Benefit runs out after 10 months, and less generous payments made to those with poor contribution records run out after 5 months.[10] This must be a major reason why only 10 per cent of unemployed Swedes have been out of work for over a year, and only 3 per cent of the whole Swedish work force is out of work.

When Beveridge wrote his Report, which established the modern social security system, he clearly had something similar in mind. He proposed that 'unemployment benefit will continue at the same rate without means test so long as unemployment lasts, but will normally be subject to a condition of attendance at a work or training centre after a certain period'. . . . 'The normal period of unconditional unemployment benefit will be six months'.[11] He believed that after that 'complete idleness even on an income demoralizes'.[12]

The main attractions of denying income support to the long-term unemployed who refuse work placements is that it would, to a very large extent, eliminate long-term unemployment. As Beveridge pointed out, it is not clear whether it is in the interests of the unemployed to be allowed to degenerate at home rather than be faced with some kind of challenge, especially if two or three alternative jobs could be offered. But there are three main problems with the proposal. First, it will be called slave labour. This is what happened when Mr. Tebbit proposed to stop paying Supplementary Benefit to young people eligible for the Youth Training Scheme. In that case the Manpower Services Commission opposed Mr. Tebbit because they did not want rebellious youngsters on their scheme. The situation is somewhat different when it comes to adults. But there is still the problem of the psychologically inadequate adult. Should he or she be forced onto a project, and what would one say if he simply could not cope with it? Clearly he would have to be financially supported. But it makes more sense to support such a person via invalidity payments than via payments to the unemployed. Finally, there is the problem of the really disadvantaged areas. Can we really imagine having over one in ten of the adults in a locality engaged in these schemes? It is not a happy thought. So I shall discuss one further stimulus for the regions in the next chapter.

But the balance of the arguments in this section seems to be this. Once a job guarantee has been established and found to be working well (but only then), benefit offices should exercise their existing right to refuse benefit to people who refuse offers of placements.

WORK INCENTIVES FOR THE SHORT-TERM UNEMPLOYED

Before going on, we should complete our discussion of benefits by considering the rest of the unemployed. Do *they* face a major disincentive to work, and, if so, what can we do about it? We have already seen that there are very few people who are as well off when unemployed as when in work. But this does not mean that benefits provide no disincentive. Nickell estimates that a 10 per cent cut in benefits would reduce unemployment by 5 per cent of its former level.[13] This is nothing like a sufficient benefit to justify the suffering involved. But there is of course another way of improving incentives—to make people better off in work. This could be done relatively easily by means of an integrated tax-transfer system for working people. Under this, poor working families could get an automatic supplement in their wage packet, just as richer ones get an automatic deduction. The best scheme is that presented by the Institute of Fiscal Studies.[14] If one is worried about work incentives, one should proceed in that direction rather than by cutting benefits.

To improve work incentives and thus reduce unemployment, there is no need to improve the after-tax income of families on above-average earnings. Thus it is very wasteful to raise the income tax threshold, since this makes all families better off. It is also wasteful to increase Child Benefit. Though this is somewhat more targeted at the families with low work incentives than is a rise in tax allowance,[15] it is still not well focused. It is much better to use a specific transfer aimed at low income families. This is available in the Family Credit. Given this, the case for income tax cuts as a method of improving incentives to work is weak indeed.

One could also tighten up the 'work test' when the economy recovers. But at present the case for this is much stronger in the South of England than in the North.

CONCLUSION

We have put forward a major proposal which could more or less eliminate long-term unemployment. We have put these proposals first because they offer the most concrete hope of a quick dent in unemployment. Given the size of the crisis, they should have priority. But we must also do much more to get the regular part of the economy going again. This is discussed in the next chapter.

Summary

1. Long-term unemployment is both unfair and inefficient (since it does not restrain inflation).
2. The long-term unemployed should be guaranteed the offer of a one-year job. Since there is vital work to be done and people wanting to do it, they should be brought together.
3. One vital area is the repair and maintenance of homes, schools, hospitals and roads. The Manpower Services Commission should spend money on projects of this kind which would not otherwise be done. The projects should be managed by private contractors (or direct labour organizations), but should employ mainly long-term unemployed people.
4. Outside construction, private employers should be paid £40 a week for a year for hiring long-term unemployed people.
5. Extra one-year jobs should be created in community care and the National Health Service to be filled by long-term unemployed.
6. Once the job guarantee was working well (and *only* then), the

benefit authorities should exercise their existing right to refuse benefit to those who reject offers of placements.

7. To encourage all unemployed people to take work, there should be more generous income support for poor working families. The level of benefits should not be cut.

9

Targeting the Jobs and Upgrading the Workers

Eliminating long-term unemployment is not enough. There are other gross imbalances in our labour market which cause great economic waste and great personal misery. These are reflected in the gross disparity between the unemployment rates of different groups shown in Table 11.

Table 11. *Disparities in Unemployment rates, October 1985*

	Percentage
By skill	
Semi- and unskilled	22
Others	10
By age	
Under 18	21
18–19	25
20–24	19
25–54	11
55–59	15
By region	
Development areas	20
(mainly in the North, North-West, and Scotland)	
Intermediate areas	16
(mainly in the West Midlands, Yorkshire, and Wales)	
Unassisted areas	11
By industry	
Construction	29
Other	13
Total	14

These disparities make it very difficult to eliminate unemployment of the disadvantaged groups by general reflation. For if we reflate across the board, we shall run into major shortages of some types of labour long before we have done much to provide jobs for the disadvantaged. *The answer is to target jobs to the disadvantaged, without at the same time adding to demand for other types of labour.* This is the key principle in the management of demand. We must create more jobs for less-skilled people, for the workers in the North, for construction workers, and for the young.

The other complementary approach is to reduce the supply of disadvantaged people by getting them to train for skills or to move house. We should proceed on both fronts; neither on its own is enough.

An obvious way to increase the demand for less-skilled workers and for workers in the North is to restructure the system of National Insurance contributions in their favour. This will be our first proposal.

Turning to public expenditure, there is a clear case for more infrastructure spending—both on structural maintenance and new building. This will again raise demand for construction workers and for the less-skilled generally.

Finally, on the side of supply a better system of education and training is a major national priority. I discuss a powerful way of stimulating training at little cost to the Exchequer, as well as other reforms.

RESTRUCTURING THE TAX ON JOBS[1]

Unemployment has always been much higher for less-skilled than for skilled people. In principle there are two possible explanations for this. One is that the unemployment does not really reflect excess supply. There is, if you like, simply more voluntary unemployment of the unskilled.

One reason for this might be that for less-skilled people, income in work is lower relative to the benefits they can get if unemployed. But, if the extra unemployment of the unskilled was purely voluntary, one would expect less-skilled labour to be in as short supply as skilled labour. This is not the case. We have evidence on this, for in their Industrial Trends Survey the Confederation of British Industy regularly ask members if their output is likely to be limited over the next four months by shortages of (a) skilled labour and (b) other labour. On average over the 60s and 70s the (weighted) proportions saying yes were: shortages of skilled labour, 23 per cent: shortages of other labour, 4 per cent. The figures in 1985 were 13 and 1 respectively. So there is a clear difference in the degree of excess supply.

This means that the pattern of relative wages is wrong. The relative wage of the less-skilled is too high for them all to be employed. So how can we price the unskilled into jobs? There are two possible strategies: to try and change the relative wage structure, *or* to accept it as it is, and offset its adverse effects by subsidies. To alter the wage structure is not easy, because many trade unions quite naturally have a preference for more equal wages, since this also makes for more equal incomes. It is true that wages have become much more unequal in the last six years (probably to a degree unprecedented in this century).[2] But this has not been enough to narrow the relative unemployment rates of the different skill groups, because at the same time the less-skilled have been the worst hit by the recession. So we need a permanent change of policy that makes for a reasonable pattern of labour costs facing employers. If we had wages that cleared markets, we should have a wider spread of wages than we now have. If we cannot have that spread, let us simulate the market solution by having a wider spread of *labour costs* facing employers. This means subsidies to employers of the lower-paid, and higher taxes for employers of the higher paid. The subsidies on the low-paid would increase their employment, while the taxes on the higher paid could help ensure that there was less bidding up of wages for the skilled manpower that is fully employed and in scarce supply.

Since the high-wage groups are reasonably fully employed, it follows that their wages are more flexible than those of the lower-paid. So, even if employers had to pay higher taxes when they employed them, their employment would fall little if anything. For this reason we could increase total employment by a self-financing scheme in which employers were subsidized if they employed low-paid people and were taxed if they employed high-wage people.

The process is illustrated in Figure 25. At the original labour

cost, unemployment of less-skilled workers is well short of supply. But when this cost is reduced by means of the subsidy, their
employment increases substantially. At the same time we are
taxing skilled workers. But because their wage is flexible, their
labour market always clears: their wage falls enough to offset
the higher tax.

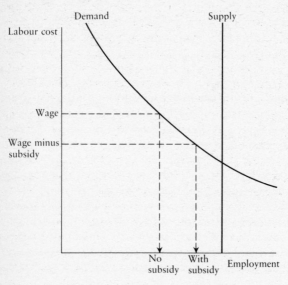

Fig. 25. Pricing Less-Skilled Workers into Jobs

The word subsidy is of course a dirty word. So, whenever
possible, one talks about a tax reduction (which is a good thing)
rather than a subsidy (which is often exactly the same thing but
sounds bad). This is easy to do in the present case—by restructuring the employers' National Insurance contributions (the
infamous tax on jobs). At present the contributions are as shown
in column (1) of Table 12. An alternative would be to eliminate
all National Insurance on earnings up to £90 a week and then
tax all earnings above that at about 24 per cent. This gives the
pattern of contributions shown in column (2). The total revenue
raised by both schemes is the same, but the second bears much

less heavily on the less-skilled. It could transform their employment prospects and it would involve no increased tax on business. Happily the present government has understood the logic in these proposals and moved a small step in this direction in the 1985 budget. But much more drastic action is needed.

Table 12. *Restructuring Employers' National Insurance Contributions (£ per week)*

Weekly earnings	Employers' National Insurance	
	Now	*Restructured*
50	3	0
90	8	0
140	15	12
200	21	26
250	26	38

We do not know exactly what changes in employment would flow from such a measure. But it is likely that a fall of 8 per cent in the cost of less-skilled labour (say, from £98 to £90) would increase demand for such workers by up to 16 per cent.[3] These are powerful effects. The effect of the whole operation could of course be further increased if it were not made self-financing. There would be a boost from the side of aggregate demand as well as from the releasing of a supply constraint.

I have mentioned the main advantages of the proposal. These come from its ability to offset some of the distortions involved in present arrangements. But there are of course other new distortions which the scheme introduces. These are much less than the advantages of the scheme, but they have to be faced.

First, though the average firm would still pay the same rate of tax, industries employing skilled work-forces might have higher labour costs (depending on how skilled wages respond), while those employing less-skilled work-forces would certainly have lower costs. Is this a bad thing? It sounds bad to be subsidizing textiles, hotels, catering, retail distribution, cleaning, and so on. But is it? After all, we are trying to mimic the effect which would follow if the wage distribution were right. If less-skilled wages were lower, we *would* have more textile, hotel, catering, and retail distribution employment. These are sectors where employment has been growing rapidly in the US. If we are serious about re-employing the mass of less-skilled workers, it is no good thinking that the only deserving industries are high tech.

Second, the real wages of the unskilled workers might adjust up in response to the increased demand for their labour. This could happen, but would be most unlikely to offset the employment-creating effects of the proposal to any great extent. In fact the reverse could happen, with unskilled wages falling. This would happen if the real rigidity is in the *ratio* of less-skilled to skilled wages, since the higher tax on skilled workers would cause a fall in their real wages.

Third, the proposal will probably reduce the incentive for people to get trained. One way to encourage people to get trained is to keep the unemployment rate of the untrained high. However it is not a nice way to do it, and other incentives are preferable. Of course if the proposal reduced differentials, this would further reduce the incentive to train. In any situation of this kind there is an inherent conflict between the objective of fully using existing resources and promoting a high rate of resource development. But it is easy to exaggerate the importance of unemployment as an incentive to train, and hard to argue that, on that count, one should not try to do something about it.

This is the main restructuring of the jobs tax that I wish to suggest. But we must, if possible, do more for the regions. Here I would suggest a marginal employment subsidy specifically for the 'assisted' areas. All increases in employment could be exempt from National Insurance contributions. The last Labour government introduced a marginal employment subsidy called the Small Firms Employment Subsidy for small firms in development areas. The evaluation suggested that it was working well, with about 40 per cent of the subsidized jobs being ones that were created as a result of the subsidy.[4]

The scheme was set for a major expansion but it was closed down by the incoming Conservative administration in 1979. We need to revive it. If we abolished the jobs tax on new jobs in 'assisted' areas, this would cost about £0.3 billion gross.[5] One could alternatively have a more ambitious scheme. For if we only subsidize new jobs, there is no incentive for firms contracting employment to contract less. However one can easily give them an incentive by subsidizing all employment greater than, for example, 90 per cent of last year's employment. This will provide an incentive to almost all firms to employ more labour than they otherwise would. But this would cost a lot more (£0.7 billion a year gross).

INFRASTRUCTURE INVESTMENT

All the proposals so far have involved subsidies or cuts in taxes, or special programmes. There has been no proposal for 'ordinary public expenditure'. Yet we know that in some fields more expenditure is desperately needed. The most obvious is the heavy end of structural maintenance, house-building and road improvements. All these involve skills and capital costs on a scale unsuited to a scheme directed specifically at the long-term unemployed.

There is a straightforward efficiency case for spending, say, an extra £1 billion on them. But, as we have seen, there is also a more sophisticated case. For infrastructure investment satisfies three of our criteria for priorities very well. It is well targeted towards construction workers and the less-skilled generally. It has a lower cost per job than general tax cuts. And it mostly goes on private-sector jobs.

UPGRADING THE WORKERS

The policies we have outlined so far constitute a major attempt to target new jobs towards types of labour with high unemployment rates. The other way to reduce the mismatch in the system and thus reduce the NAIRU is to alter the pattern of workers available. Let us go back to our earlier discussion of mismatch. Figure 26 illustrates an imbalance between the pattern of labour demand and labour supply. (Labour demand is employment plus vacancies, and labour supply is employment plus unemployment). There are two ways to improve the alignment. One is to retarget the jobs to where the workers are available. This is what we have been doing so far (while at the same time increasing the total number of jobs). The other approach is to switch the workers out of the categories that are in excess supply. This means essentially training them for skills and getting them to move out of the regions of high unemployment. We should do both.

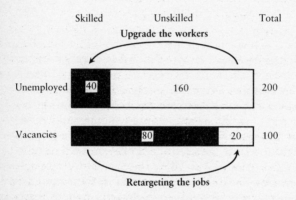

Fig. 26. Two Ways to Improve Matching.

It is of vital importance that the skill levels of the British population be improved. We do not in this country have natural resources as abundantly as in many countries. But Japan, Israel, Hong Kong, and Singapore have shown how countries without great natural resources can prosper if they develop their human resources. We are currently not doing this well. There are at least three major areas of failure (starting at the bottom).

First, there is the low level of numeracy acquired in school. Mathematical and logical reasoning is central to much economic activity. Yet in Britain only a quarter of all pupils get 'O' level mathematics, compared with over a half getting the equivalent in Germany. Turning to the less able half of our pupils their numeracy is two years less advanced than in Germany. In fact the average numeracy of the 'bottom half' in Germany seems to be about the same as the overall average in Britain![6] The most obvious reason for this is that many of those who teach maths in our schools are quite unprepared for the task. In secondary schools, under half of those teaching mathematics have maths as the main subject of their highest qualification. Over a quarter do not have mathematics as even a subsidiary subject in their higher education.[7]

The only way to deal with this problem is to treat it as a crisis. We should say that only teachers with a Certificate of Competence to Teach Mathematics should be allowed to do so. (This could be a different certificate for primary and for secondary school teaching). This could not be introduced overnight. Instead we should announce now that this will be required from, say, 1992 onwards.

This announcement would set in motion a whole train of events. Existing teachers of maths would clamour for courses to give them the certificate. Those with no gift for the subject would go elsewhere. Some teachers who do not now teach maths would see new openings for their talents, and would take conversion courses. Existing teachers with suitable maths qualifications and good teaching records would of course be given the certificate without taking a course. This whole process would certainly cost money, but the cost would not be large relative to the education budget, nor relative to the benefits it would generate. We cannot hope to have a decent living standard and to compete in international markets unless we decide now to be as numerate as the Germans.

We are also letting our youngsters down when they leave school. At the graduate level we do badly compared with the US and Japan but much the same as Germany.[8] However our real failure is at the sub-degree level. The British labour force is dreadfully polarized in education (as in social attitudes). There is the group with higher education and the group with minimum education, and deplorably few in between. This is illustrated by Table 13, which shows the distribution of qualifications in the British and German labour force.

The difference comes from two sources. First, we have far fewer people continuing in full-time education in their late teens than in most other advanced countries. This is illustrated in the

Table 13. *Labour Force Qualifications in Britain and Germany*

Qualification	Britain (%)	Germany (%)
University level	6	7
Other (including apprenticeships completed)	30	60
None	64	33
	100	100

following figures, which show the proportion of those aged 16–18 (inclusive) in full-time education.[9]

USA	79%
Japan	69%
France	58%
Germany	45%
UK	32%

Second, there is the comparative role of part-time training. Traditionally, most of the skilled work-force and technicians educated in Britain have come up the part-time route through apprenticeships. Even in the 1970s, however, this was less well-developed here than in Germany, with under half as many people completing apprenticeships.[10] But since 1979 the apprenticeship system here has been really clobbered by the recession. For example in the engineering industry the number of new craft and technician trainees averaged around 25,000 in the 1970s. Since 1979, the numbers have fallen as follows:[11]

1978/79	25,000
1979/80	23,000
1980/81	20,000
1981/82	15,000
1982/83	11,000
1983/84	9,000
1984/85	9,000

At the same time regular youth employment has plummeted.

The response to this has been the government's Youth Training Scheme. Since 1978, the government has offered a guaranteed place on a programme to all 16-year olds. This was originally called the Youth Opportunities Programme (YOP), but was converted into a more ambitious Youth Training Scheme (YTS) in 1983. This currently provides for a one-year programme. Most of the places are based in firms but the employee has to guarantee at least 13 weeks in the year off-the-job training. This can be in a college or a workshop on the firm's premises. The trainee is paid £27.30 a week from Manpower Services Commission funds, and in addition the firm gets roughly £10 a week towards its other costs. In January 1986, 340,000 young people were on this scheme.

As Table 14 shows, these schemes have provided for an increasing number of young people. They will provide for even more when the Youth Training Scheme is expanded during 1986 to provide a two-year programme involving a minimum of 20 weeks' off-the-job training in the two years.

But two major deficiencies remain. First, many young people still take jobs which involve no formal training. Of young employees in the table, only a third were receiving any formal off-the-job training.[12] To deal with this problem we should

Table 14. *Activities of 16- and 17-year olds, January (per cent)*

	Full-time education	YOP/ YTS	Employees	Unemployed	All
16-year olds					
1980	42	6	46	6	100
1981	43	11	34	12	100
1982	47	14	27	12	100
1983	48	19	19	14	100
1984	46	24	18	12	100
1985	46	28	13	13	100
17-year olds					
1980	25	2	64	9	100
1981	29	4	54	13	100
1982	28	5	50	17	100
1983	31	8	44	17	100
1984	31	5	46	18	100
1985	31	4	48	17	100

require, as in Germany, that all young employees aged under 18 be released for at least eight hours' off-the-job training a week.

The second deficiency which still remains to be tackled is mainly at the technician and professional levels. The demand for craftsmen is, if anything, falling. But the demand for technicians is booming, and considerable skill shortages exist at this level. For example, of 2,000 companies surveyed by the CBI in 1984, 57 per cent reported 'difficulty in filling jobs which required certain skills, qualification, or experience'.[13] Those experiencing difficulties were then asked to identify the areas affected: 54 per cent mentioned professional staff, 52 per cent mentioned technicians, and 42 per cent mentioned skilled workers. They were also asked how these problems could best be solved. Only 13 per cent mentioned the Youth Training Scheme, 35 per cent schools, 68 per cent further education, and (biggest of all) 71 per cent mentioned in-company training.

So there seems to be a major need for better incentives for companies to undertake training at the post YTS stage. By far the best framework in which to develop specific skills is in employment. Detailed full-time vocational training in college is often wasted because the individual then finds that he cannot get a job that uses that particular skill, or that he does not like that type of work. Much better to get into a job and then acquire the skill. Moreover this also improves the motivation to learn.

So we have to rely upon employers as the prime determinants of the amount of training that happens. They are the best placed to judge what kinds of specific training are most needed. But their judgements on how *much* training is needed are often woefully defective. There are many reasons why too little training is likely to happen if the matter is left entirely to the market.[14] For example, firms will undertrain if they fear that other firms will pinch their trainees the moment they are qualified. So the government must intervene to provide additional incentives for training.

The 1964 Industrial Training Act tried to do this by a system of levies and rebates. Within each industry, the Industrial Training Board decided what proportion of the wage-bill each firm should be required to pay in levy. Firms were then rebated whatever money they spent on training up to the level of their levy contribution, the Boards spending the remainder. Over time more and more firms came to be rebated all their levy, because the levy had not kept in step with firms' voluntary decisions. Hence the levy/rebate system largely ceased to have any effect. This was one reason why the ITBs lost credibility and some have now been abolished.

A new system of finance is needed—one that is as unbureaucratic as possible. What incentive lever can be operated, which involves the minimum of bureaucratic apparatus? The following 'marginal' subsidy would work well. Each factory or establishment would be classified according to its industry.[15] Within each industry the government would each year compute the 'average training share', i.e. the ratio of training expenditures (not including trainees' salaries) to total wage-bill. Then, in the following year each establishment which spent on training more than the 'average training share' would have all its excess expenditure rebated from public funds. Any establishment that spent less than that share would pay a tax equal to its underspending. Every firm would therefore have an incentive to increase its spending on training. By this method the total percentage of the national wage-bill spent on training would be induced to rise year by year for some years. But the cost to public funds would be small, since in any year the government would only pay for the cost of any *increased* real expenditure by firms. The proposed rebate-cum-tax would of course be self-assessed by establishments, and the administrative cost would consist mainly of the cost of spot checks.

MOVING BETWEEN REGIONS

It is as important that workers should be in the right place as that they should have the right skills. The housing market is the basic obstacle here. The main problem of course is that rents are not set at levels which clear the market. If an American is unemployed and hears there are jobs in Texas, he never thinks for a minute about whether he could find a place to live. He just goes. The same is true for most parts of America, except for a few like New York City which have rent control. So changes in the direction of more flexible rents are essential. But we also need better administrative procedures for council house swaps and a bigger reserved quota of council houses for migrants.[16] Perhaps all youngsters from high unemployment areas should also be given a week's career-oriented holiday in a lower unemployment area. How else are we to get young people to move to where the jobs are?[17]

We must also get the employment service to provide more information in the depressed areas about jobs in areas where there is a shortage of labour. Welsh unemployment in the 1930s was eased by massive migration into Slough, and similar movements are now becoming inevitable.

Summary

1. We need to eliminate the jobs tax on unskilled workers. This could be partly paid for by higher taxes on skilled labour, designed to prevent overheating in the skilled market.
2. We should eliminate the jobs tax on new jobs created in the depressed areas.
3. We should spend more on infrastructure investment.
4. We should improve education and training. Maths teachers should require a certificate of competence. Every worker under 18 should receive at least eight hours a week training off-the-job. And there should be a new rebate-cum-tax scheme to induce firms to spend a lot more on training.
5. The housing market should be made more flexible to stimulate mobility between regions.

10

A Viable Incomes Policy

To restore employment, we need more, well-targeted spending, and a better-qualified labour force. But, however much targeting and however improved the labour force, there is the ever present menace of a wage explosion. If we want to reduce unemployment to the levels of the late 1970s, there is no hope without an incomes policy. And we have to have a policy that can last.

So let us first look at the history of incomes policy, which has good and bad parts. Then I shall argue that conventional policies, though better than none, cannot last. The alternative is a tax-based approach. This would give the flexibility needed for permanence, and it would be administratively feasible.

INCOMES POLICY IN THE LATER 1970s

The starting point in thinking about incomes policy is the history of the later 1970s. For in retrospect it is clear that we could not have had unemployment at only $1\frac{1}{4}$ million then unless we had had an incomes policy. Thus much can be learned from both the successes and failures of that period.

When the Labour party came to power in March 1974, the first oil shock had just occurred. This pushed up prices rapidly. Until August, wages responded automatically under the 'threshold' provisions enacted by the Heath government. But the Labour government itself had no incomes policy except a loose 'social contract' with the trade union movement, which said that settlements should be roughly in line with the cost of living. As a result, wage inflation continued to escalate, reaching a peak of 30 per cent over a 12-month period. But then an incomes policy was introduced. From August 1975–6 there was a ceiling of £6 a week per person (equivalent to 10 per cent growth for a person on average earnings). From August 1976–7 there was a 5 per cent ceiling. These two policies were supported by the TUC, and reserve powers had been prepared for use should settlements not follow the policy. In any case, employers were not legally allowed to pass on into prices any wage increase going beyond the policy. In the event nearly all settlements conformed to the policy. The effect was remarkable, as can be seen from Figure 11 and Table 15. Whereas wages had increased by 26 per cent in the year up to August 1975, they increased by only 7 per cent in the year up to August 1977. Thus it is not surprising that econometric wage equations estimate that the first year's incomes policy reduced inflation by 13 per cent per annum.[1] Thanks to this, the government was not forced to deflate the economy, which would have been the only other way to control inflation.

From August 1977 the TUC ceased to provide official support for incomes policy, though it did not support breaches of it. The policy on the other hand continued to be supported by the sanction of withdrawal of public contracts from employers who did not conform. The norm for 1977–8 was 10 per cent, and for 1978–9 it was 5 per cent, though the government fell (over Scottish devolution) before the year was out. From 1977 onwards more settlements than before directly breached the

Table 15. *Wage Inflation and Incomes Policy in the 1970s*

	Incomes policy	Change in average weekly earnings (%)	
		Prescribed by the policy	Actual
November 1972–April 1973	Freeze	0	1.8
April 1973–November 1973	£1 + 4% (£5 max.)	6.7	10.3
November 1973–August 1974	£2.25 or 7% (£7 max.) + 'threshold'	13.0	14.9
August 1974–August 1975	No limit	No limit	25.9
August 1975–August 1976	£6	10.4	14.3
August 1976–August 1977	5% (£2.50 min; £4 max.)	4.5	7.3
August 1977–August 1978	10%	10.0	13.9

policy. Some people have argued that, as the policy collapsed, all the gains that had been achieved in the earlier phase were lost, so that the inflation rate had not in the long run been changed by the policy. But the best evidence in fact suggests that the 'catch-up' from the collapse of the incomes policy was negligible.[2]

Four factors accounted for the rise in wage inflation to a peak of 26 per cent in September 1980 (over September 1979). First, there was the tighter labour market of 1978–9. Then there was the second oil price rise in 1979—and with it the rise in other commodity prices, pushing up prices generally. Third, there was the rise in Value Added Tax from 8 per cent to 15 per cent in the first Conservative Budget in May 1979. And finally there was the total abandonment of incomes policy.

Since 1979 the government has had no incomes policy. It has of course had a public sector incomes policy, but every government has had that since before Nebuchadnezzar. Public sector incomes policy is of course essential but it is not a major weapon in the fight against inflation. Over any longish period, public sector pay is bound to grow at much the same rate as private sector pay in order to maintain recruitment, retention, and morale. Public sector wage inflation will be 'comparable' to private sector wage inflation.

The key issue is: How is private sector wage inflation determined? The best evidence is that private sector wage inflation causes public sector wage inflation (via comparability and via its effect on prices), whereas the effect of public sector wage inflation (other than in the nationalized industries) upon private sector wage inflation is small.[3]

So it is extremely confusing when people say that a government already has an 'incomes policy' if it has a public sector incomes policy. For the incomes policy which matters is that for the private sector. The present government has no such policy, and is extremely proud of the fact. It seems quite unaware that this may be a major reason for Britain's weaker economic performance since the 1970s.

A few simple figures illustrate this point. The best way to evaluate our performance is to measure our key variables as differences from OECD averages. (This eliminates the effect of the common external shocks to which all OECD countries have been subject.) Since any government inherits an inflation rate, the best measure of inflation performance is the change in inflation. On the output side we shall take unemployment as the best indicator of whether we are using our resources properly. Under the Labour government [1974 (4th quarter) to 1979 (2nd quarter)], unemployment was close to the average for the rest of the OECD.[4] Price inflation was reduced by 7 per cent in Britain and by 5 per cent in the OECD.[5] So Britain was doing at least as well as the OECD—with some help from incomes policy. Under the Conservative government [1979 (2nd quarter) to 1985 (2nd quarter)], our unemployment has been way above the OECD average—11 per cent on average over the period compared to 7 per cent. Yet our inflation has come down no more than the OECD average (4 per cent in each case). So Britain's trade-off between inflation and unemployment has worsened dramatically relative to other countries. One reason must be our abandonment of incomes policy.

So what is to be done? We cannot go on using unemployment as the only weapon against inflation. We must find some other instrument, so that we can get unemployment down.

CONVENTIONAL INCOMES POLICY

There are two broad options that seem practically feasible.[6] One is the kind of policy operated in the 1970s. Under this, the growth in pay for each type of worker is centrally determined. It may be a flat rate increase or a percentage one or something more subtly differentiated. But it comes from the centre, either as a result of a deal between the TUC and the government (as in the later 1970s) or by government fiat (as under Mr Heath). Though this kind of policy is in my view far better than no incomes policy, it involves three major problems.

First, free collective bargaining is in effect suspended, since settlements have to conform to externally imposed rules. People are willing to accept this kind of thing for a while, but eventually they rebel against external regulation of something they consider a basic human right. This is the right to settle wages by bargaining between the employer and the worker. For this reason it is politically impossible and also undesirable for a centrally regulated incomes policy to be permanent. And yet it is essential to have a permanent incomes policy if we are to get a sufficient reduction in the NAIRU.

A second problem with conventional incomes policies is that, if they are to persist, they have to provide some mechanism for the adjustment of relativities. This must involve the ruling of a central body. But it is extremely difficult for any central body to get enough information to give sensible rulings on the thousands of cases that have to be decided. From reading the newspapers one is apt not to realize how many settlements there are. In Britain today two-thirds of workers have their pay settled by bargaining with their individual employers.[7] An effective supervision of this number of settlements is virtually out of the question, except in a crude way for a short period.

Third, there is the problem of the link between settlements and actual pay. Clearly it is actual earnings paid out that determine the cost of labour and hence ultimately the prices in the shops. And yet it is now increasingly difficult for an outsider to tell how earnings will actually be affected by any particular settlement. This is because an increasing part of earnings consists of payments-by-results and other formulae. So incomes policies which are designed to bear on settlements may have only a limited impact on earnings.

For these three reasons, conventional incomes policies, though they may work for short periods of time, are not really feasible on a permanent basis. An alternative is an incomes policy that works by general incentives rather than by the regulation of individual cases. This means using the tax system to discourage an excessive growth of wages. Many detailed schemes have been put forward for a 'counter-inflation tax' but I shall confine myself to the following version.[8]

A COUNTER-INFLATION TAX

Each year the government should declare a norm for the growth of average hourly earnings. If a firm controls the growth of average hourly pay to this level, it is subject to no tax penalty. But if it goes above the norm, it pays a tax on all its excess wage payments. For example, suppose the norm was 2 per cent and a firm paid a 5 per cent growth in average hourly earnings. It would be taxed on the 3 per cent difference. So if the tax rate was 100 per cent, the firm's tax liability would equal roughly 3 per cent of its total wage bill (to be precise, 3/105ths of it). The tax would reduce the rate of wage increase at a given level of unemployment. To make sure that price increases were similarly reduced, the government would ensure that the total burden of taxes on firms as a whole was not increased. The general rate of National Insurance contributions on all firms would be cut by an amount equal to the proceeds of the counter-inflation tax.

Compare an arrangement like this with a centralized incomes policy. First, there is no absolute compulsion on anybody. Free collective bargaining continues. Firms and workers can agree on pay rises above the norm, but they are discouraged from going too far by the tax. If a group is paid above the norm, the policy has not broken down, nor is the policy or the government discredited. Though the government would aim to agree the policy with the unions, it could if necessary impose it without their agreement. So we have a policy that can be permanent. Second, the adjustment of relativities is determined in a decentralized manner through collective bargaining, and not by a central pay body. This should appeal to all those who believe that excessive centralism is one of the basic evils of our day. And finally, the tax bears on actual pay and not on notional settlements.

This seems to me to make it superior to the policies of the 1970s. Since it is also less familiar, I shall spend the rest of the chapter discussing it in more detail.

EFFECTS[9]

How would a counter-inflation tax reduce the NAIRU? To reduce the NAIRU, we know from Chapter 3 that we have to reduce the degree of real wage pressure at a given level of unemployment. This then makes it possible to run the economy at a higher level of employment. We reproduce the relevant diagram in Figure 27. If there is less wage pressure, there will be less unemployment.

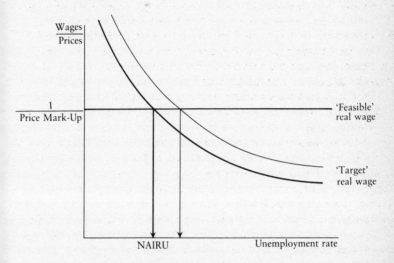

Fig. 27. How the NAIRU Can Be Reduced.

So how exactly would a counter-inflation tax reduce wage pressure? Most wages are set by bargaining between firms and unions. So we can see how the tax works by seeing how it affects the motivation of firms and of unions. If firms are powerless, the unions' aspect will be the more important, and vice versa.

Let us start with firms. Individual firms left to themselves would not pay their workers nothing. For they need to be able to attract, retain, and motivate their workers. So firms have some incentive to pay higher than their rivals. Only when unemployment is high enough will such leap-frogging cease. Thus many observers are surprised nowadays that private employers are paying wages that grow at around 8 per cent a year, when the unions are so weak in the private sector due to high unemployment. The answer must be that firms are keen to keep up with the Joneses, and at current levels of unemployment they are not in the mood to reduce wage inflation.

But suppose there were a stiff wage-inflation tax equal to, say, 100 per cent of all wage increases over 5 per cent. Then a firm could save 4 per cent of its wage bill by sticking to the norm rather than paying a 9 per cent wage increase. A firm with a wage bill of £1 million would thus save £40,000. Compared with a profit of, say, £100,000 (excluding depreciation), this saving would not be sneezed at. So employers would have a strong incentive to pay lower wages at given unemployment. If the government did not supply the extra demand for output, inflation would start falling. Alternatively the government could reflate the economy, and thus offset the new downward pressure on wages. In this case the economy would have moved to a lower NAIRU at the same level of inflation. Either outcome would be a lot better than what we have now.

Let us turn now to the other case and see how the counter-inflation tax would affect unions. If individual unions had the right to choose their own wages, they would not choose unlimited wage increases. For they know that employers cannot be forced to employ workers, and the individual employer will lose business if his workers cost too much. So unions choose their wage targets, knowing that higher wages mean fewer jobs. Given this constraint, there is some ideal wage that they have in mind.

How will this change if a wage-inflation tax is introduced? If wages are pushed up, this costs the employer a lot more with the tax than without it. For example, if the inflation tax is at 100 per cent, a £1 wage increase above the norm will cost the employer £2. This makes it much more likely that the employer will have to lay off workers or close down. So the unions will push less hard on the wages front under a wage-inflation tax. They will behave as if they care more about jobs relative to employment.

In the economists' jargon, the tax increases the elasticity of demand for labour. But union monopoly power depends entirely on the demand for labour being as inelastic as possible. Thus the tax effectively reduces the monopoly power of the unions.

It is important to note that if the scheme is made fiscally neutral, a wage increase for one group will not reduce *total* employment, but it will reduce employment of the group concerned. Thus there is an incentive for the individual group to settle for lower wages.

WAGES IN THE PUBLIC SECTOR

The counter-inflation tax would be confined to the private sector and the nationalized industries. Does this mean that it would have no effect in central and local government? Far from it. They would benefit from the tax in three important ways. First, if comparability is used as an argument in public sector pay settlements, any scheme which helps in the private sector must contribute to the problem of public sector pay. This is crucial. There is a strong tendency to suppose that settlements in the public sector somehow determine the national inflation rate. But, as we have said, there is no evidence of this.[10] Broadly, private sector pay is determined by economic conditions in the private sector. Public sector pay follows private sector pay.

Moreover, if private sector wages are held down by the tax, this will also restrain prices. As we know, the cost of living, as well as comparability, has an important influence on public sector pay.

Finally, an economy-wide norm would provide a useful frame of reference in public pay negotiations. In central and local government there could be a presumption that workers get the norm plus a catch-up equal to the difference between last year's private sector pay growth and last year's norm. (This formula could be modified to allow extra increases for government employees whose occupation was in shortage or whose comparator group had grown faster than the private sector average. Any extra payments of this type would of course be deducted when calculating the catch-up.) In this way average pay in government and the private sector would grow in line.[11]

In the nationalized industries the tax might have an additional effect through the incentive it provided to employers to resist wage increases (just as in the private sector). This incentive would obviously not hold if it were known that the industry's external financing limit, which the government imposes, would be increased to pay the tax; and doubtless this would sometimes occur. Thus it may be that the tax would have little direct effect on miners' pay. But it would profoundly affect all public pay (even that of miners) through its effect on private sector wages and prices.

THE INTRODUCTION OF THE TAX

Of course a key issue is how the tax is introduced, for this will have a big effect on its credibility. For technical reasons the tax could not come into force on the day it was announced. For it is a tax on wage growth, and can only be levied once firms have been collecting data on appropriately defined wage payments for at least a year. This suggests the following strategy. A government would simultaneously announce a conventional incomes policy (say, a percentage limit on wage settlements) to last for, say, 18 months. It would also announce that after 18 months this policy would be replaced by a counter-inflation tax. When the 18 months were up, the public would welcome the greater flexibility to adjust differentials and redress anomalies that the tax would permit. But they would also think of the counter-inflation tax as a modification of a more familiar type of incomes policy, which would add to the credibility of the tax.

The point about the time lag is important. At present the Alliance parties in Britain are committed to putting a counter-inflation tax on the statute book as soon as they come into government, for use if it proved necessary. At a minimum this law should provide for immediate collection of the relevant data. In fact I have no doubt that the tax will be necessary, and it would be much better if the British people were to face this reality now rather than when an expansionary policy runs into trouble.

GAINERS AND LOSERS

It is natural to ask who gains and who loses from the tax. Clearly, the unemployed gain from anything that increases employment. But would a counter-inflation tax also benefit those who already have work? A common argument against incomes policy is that it will lower the living standards of workers.

This is misleading. If prices are essentially a mark-up on wages, then in the long-run, if wages are lower, prices are lower. Living standards are unaffected.

There are two qualifications to this, against each of which there are offsetting considerations. First, if wages are held down, prices do not immediately fall, and real wages can be temporarily reduced.[12] But this assumes that the point of the tax is to reduce inflation. I would prefer to see it used to contain inflation at a steady level as we reflate the economy.

Second qualification: It may be true that higher employment would be associated with higher prices relative to costs (a point we discussed in Ch. 3). But this need not mean that workers are less well-off, for two reasons. First, we are proposing some tax cuts, so that wages will be a higher fraction of costs.[13] Second, more life in the economy will lead to more investment, and hence a higher capital stock. That is bound to raise real wages.

So workers have nothing to fear from a properly constructed incomes policy. One can understand why unions worry about a conventional incomes policy which deprives them of their bargaining rights. But they should welcome a more flexible policy instrument that offers the prospect of work to hundreds of thousands who would otherwise be out of work.

One understands the unions' political difficulties in accepting any incomes policy. They must be fully involved in the design of the policy and in annual discussions of the norm, which should be based on a national economic assessment. There should also for political reasons be a similar tax on dividend income, using the same norm and again offset by an equivalent nation-wide cut in the jobs tax. But in the final event it would be intolerable if union leaders blocked an incomes policy and forced the government yet again to use unemployment as the only weapon against inflation.

AN ADMINISTRATIVE NIGHTMARE?

But is a counter-inflation tax administratively feasible? When I first thought about this question, I thought that it might be quite difficult to administer. Happily, further study has shown that it can be relatively straightforward.

First, *the method of collection*. The tax would be paid to the Inland Revenue once a quarter. Each firm would calculate its own liability, as it does with Pay As You Earn Income Tax (PAYE) and National Insurance (NI) contributions. It would then just send off a cheque to the relevant computer centre. It would also complete a brief pro-forma giving total earnings and man-hours, in justification of its assessed liability.

Firms have of course an incentive to lie over this tax, as they do over PAYE and NI payments. They would therefore be subject to spot audit at one week's notice (as with PAYE and NI). At present the audit of the whole of PAYE and NI at the firms' end requires under five hundred inspectors, so there is no reason why the audit of the counter-inflation tax should require more than one hundred or so.

Next, *the coverage of the tax*. In the private sector it could be confined to companies employing over 100 workers. This would mean that under 20,000 companies were involved, compared with nearly a million pay-points for PAYE. This would save greatly on administrative cost both to the Revenue and to firms. Most of the firms affected have computerized payrolls, which include the hours for which they have paid their hourly paid workers. Moreover, in large firms cheating is less likely both because firms value their reputations, and because a manager who cheated would be less likely to gain personally from the firm's cheating.

One might think at first blush that, if small firms were exempt, this would lead to everyone wanting to become a small firm. But this would not happen provided that whatever adjustment was made to the rate of National Insurance contributions (discussed earlier) applied only to firms which were liable for the counter-inflation tax.

How would the norm be set? It should of course be discussed with the TUC and CBI but it would ultimately be the government's responsibility, as are all taxes. The level of the norm would be a matter of judgement and would have to be consistent with the policy on aggregate demand. One would hope that it could be held fairly steady, with price inflation rather than wage inflation varying to reflect changes in the price of imports relative to domestic costs.

Next, *the tax base*. This is average hourly earnings. For simplicity earnings would be measured exactly as they are for Income Tax purposes (PAYE). It would be impracticable to include any fringe benefits not included in PAYE earnings. But if fringe benefits do increase relative to PAYE earnings, it is hard to see how in any one year, fringe-inclusive earnings growth could exceed fringe-exclusive growth by more than a fraction of 1 percentage point. And what about the measurement of hours? Where pay varies with hours worked, it would be hours-paid-for; in the case of other workers it would be counted as 35 hours a week (full time) and 20 hours (part time).

The tax would be levied at *the level of the firm*. Totally new enterprises would be excluded. But there might be problems connected with changes in the ownership of existing enterprises. These can be handled provided it is understood that, wherever there has been continuous economic activity, that activity is deemed to have a past.

There are doubtless many ways in which firms will try to evade the tax. But this is true of all taxes. People tend to assume that the taxes we already have are securely founded, while any new ones are insecure in the extreme. But, when one looks into it, it seems that a counter-inflation tax could be quite straightforward. It would be much less of a bureaucratic nightmare than a prolonged conventional incomes policy.

ECONOMIC COSTS

So far I have praised the tax. The time has come to face up to the problems involved. But these problems must always be seen in perspective. In later life Maurice Chevalier was asked what he thought of old age. 'It's not so bad,' he replied, 'when you consider the alternative.'

The alternative to a counter-inflation tax must be at least 2 per cent more of the work-force unemployed. This means a loss of at least £6,000 million in output plus untold human suffering and degradation. So when one considers the inevitable costs of any kind of intervention, one must weigh them against the very major benefits.

The costs are certainly substantial. The most obvious one is the discouragement of productivity deals. If a firm wants to buy out overmanning or to persuade workers to accept new machinery, it generally has to offer a quid pro quo. If on top of that quid pro quo it has to pay the Chancellor an equivalent amount, the firm will be less inclined to go for the deal. But how many deals would actually flounder for this reason? After all, the tax is only paid in the year of the deal, while the benefits to the firm and the workers last long after. Suppose a fifth of productivity deals get postponed. Is this a cost worth bearing for, say, 3 per cent lower unemployment and £9 billion more output? I think so. However, if one is still worried about this, one could exempt from the tax any extra payments to workers that arise from a profit-sharing scheme and were also accompanied by an increase in shareholders' profits. One could not exempt any other form of profit-share payments from the scope of the tax without totally undermining its effectiveness.[14]

The other cost of the tax is that it penalizes the firm that is upgrading its work-force. This sounds really bad. But, as I have said earlier, it is the less skilled who are unemployed and who need to be subsidized. So this form of subsidization can't really do much harm. High tech can to a large extent look after itself. As the Chancellor has pointed out, we shall never beat unemployment if we despise 'no tech' and the people whose best chance of a job is in that kind of work.

WHAT ABOUT LOW PAY?

Some people believe that the main argument for incomes policy is that it enables you to kill two birds with one stone—to control inflation *and* to alter the structure of pay to help those who are worst off. But unfortunately one stone aimed at two birds often misses both. The inclusion of the flat-rate element in the policy of 1975–6 set up tensions which helped to destroy incomes policy later in the 1970s. And it did little to redistribute income.[15] But, more important, the connection between family poverty and low pay is not particularly close.[16] So it is much better to deal with poverty through the Budget than through wages policy.[17]

WHY NOT CONTROL PRICES DIRECTLY?

Some would of course argue that, if we want to control price inflation, we should not bother about wages at all but should rather control prices. But there are major problems with direct controls on prices. First, it is very difficult to measure prices when the quality of the product can be changed and when new products are constantly coming into existence. These problems are much less severe with different qualities of labour. Second, the prices of different goods grow (and should grow) at very different rates, whereas the wages of different types of worker grow (and should grow) at fairly similar rates. Because of differences in productivity growth, we expect the price of electronic calculators to fall, and the price of haircuts to rise in line with wages. One could not contemplate any policy that treated all price increases on the same lines. So prices policy means allowing firms to charge prices which give them a reasonable profit margin on top of the cost of wages and raw materials.

But what is 'reasonable'? In the late 1970s the rule was the margin prevailing in the best three of the last five years. Even with such a procedure there is endless room for argument over the measurement of profit, depending on the treatment of capital cost. Price control is thus bound to involve a major bureaucratic apparatus. If it is effective, control on margins may in many cases discourage investment. But it will equally often be ineffective. Many firms would argue that under it they push up their prices faster than they otherwise would, in order to establish a nice high base in case the next bureaucrat next year is tougher than this year's bureaucrat.

So any attempt to control prices is likely to be either inefficient or ineffective. It seems best to keep clear of it. Because of the difficulties of measurement, a price code is not even likely to be a very good method of enforcing regulations on wages.

But if we control wages directly, we *are* also controlling price inflation. For the long-run growth of prices will be the same as of wages (apart from productivity change, terms of trade change, and changes in distributive shares). Anyone who puts out figures showing that wages and prices over some short term have moved very differently (due for example to exchange rate changes) is simply trying to confuse people. The long-run growth of prices is primarily determined by the long-run growth of domestic costs, which mainly means wages. Thus controlling wages (with a linked control on dividends) is the key to controlling inflation. And controlling inflation is the key to any major reduction in unemployment.

Summary

1. To achieve a sufficient reduction of the NAIRU, a permanent incomes policy is needed.
2. Traditional centralized incomes policies cannot be permanent because they suspend free collective bargaining, and make relativities a matter for administrative decision.
3. The answer is a policy in which there is a norm for the growth in average hourly earnings in each enterprise. If earnings grow more than this, they would be subject to a steep tax (e.g. 100 per cent) paid by the firm.
4. This would discourage firms from bidding up wages against each other and would discourage excessive pay claims from unions, because this would be more likely to bankrupt their employers and cause job loss.
5. The administration of the tax would be quite simple. The tax would be collected at the level of the enterprise (excluding

enterprises with less than 100 workers). Pay would be defined as for PAYE. The firm would assess its own tax liability (if any) as for PAYE, and send in a cheque. Audit of the scheme would require only about 100 inspectors.

6. The tax would be part of the tax law, but the norm would be discussed, and hopefully agreed, with the Trades Union Congress and employers' organizations.

11

Aggregate Demand and Sound Finance: Will the Programme Work?

We have outlined a programme to increase spending both by government (on public projects and services) and by private households. In addition there should be temporary incentives to firms to undertake investment within the next three years, in order to get the economy moving. All this will increase the budget deficit by at least 1 per cent of national income in the first year, and another 1 per cent in the second year.

Can we be sure that the extra spending will lead to extra real output, and not be dissipated in higher inflation? And, if inflation is kept in check, will this require such high interest rates that investment falls as much as other real spending increases, leaving the total number of jobs unchanged?

INFLATION VERSUS GROWTH

Let us start with the argument about inflation. We shall first address it in general terms, and then more specifically in the context of our policy.

The argument of the pessimists is that extra money spending will generate no extra jobs—only higher prices. The argument stems from the Chicago school and has been transmitted to Britain by Patrick Minford.[1] It is a major intellectual underpinning of present government policy and is reflected for example in the Chancellor's famous Mais Lecture.[2]

The argument goes like this. Suppose the government pursues a systematic policy of spending more money in depressions. Then people will know the government is doing this and will adjust prices upwards, so that there is no effect on output. The only other policy the government could pursue would be unsystematic, and that would merely increase the fluctuations in output. So economic policy can do nothing to reduce economic fluctuations.

The whole line of reasoning is very strange. It is based on a model in which depressions only occur because of errors of information. People are generally assumed not to read the newspapers, and not to have any idea about the retail price index or the money supply or indeed about whether there is a depression. They *are* however assumed to have an accurate model of the economic system, about which everybody is meant to be agreed.[3]

We could easily forget this view of the world, were it not for its widespread influence in this country. In its popular form the argument often goes like this. Over the last 20 years, money spending has risen by 12 per cent, yet output has only risen by 2 per cent. The rest has gone into prices. Thus there cannot be any lack of demand, and any extra spending we might undertake would go into prices and not output.

But the conclusion is false. It is perfectly true that over the long haul, the growth of output depends on real forces in the economy and not on the level of money spending. But a change in the *growth rate* of money spending can have profound short-term effects on output. For example between 1980 and 1984, the growth rate of money spending in Britain was cut from 17 per cent a year to 6 per cent. The government had been led to believe that this contraction would all go into prices rather than output. Mainstream economists warned them otherwise, and sure enough there was a massive contraction of output.

The US recession in 1982 was also caused by a fall in money spending. But the Americans had the sense to reverse this fall, and a higher budget deficit brought unemployment tumbling down.

The reason that an expansionary budget works is that prices are sticky, and nothing like as flexible as the Chicago school believe. Thus, when money spending changes, the extra spending does not all go into prices: much of it goes into output.

Of course, if unemployment were already below the NAIRU, there would be little point exploiting this stickiness. For, though output would rise, so would inflation, and the higher level of output would not be sustained. But if unemployment is not below the NAIRU, it makes perfect sense to expand spending and boost output, unless you are committed to still further reductions in inflation.

The preceding account is the essence of what might be called mainstream economics. I have deliberately avoided the terms 'monetarist' and 'Keynesian' because they are used to mean so many things that they now mean almost nothing. But it may be worth noting that modern mainstream economics differs from 'old-style Keynesian' in accepting the existence of a NAIRU (first posited by Friedman in 1968). But it shares with the old-style Keynesian the emphasis on sticky prices. This is why policies on aggregate demand matter. Attending to the supply side is not enough.

However, general principles on either side are a quite inadequate guide for policy. Apart from anything, we wish to ensure that our policy will not lead to *any* more inflation than would otherwise occur. How can this be done?

AVOIDING INCREASES IN INFLATION

Price inflation comes from increases in costs, that is from rises in wages or in import prices. We have already considered in detail how to avoid wage inflation and designed our policies accordingly. But how can we avoid inducing rises in import prices through a fall in the exchange rate?

Is our programme bound to precipitate a run on the pound? The answer is, Not at all. It all depends on what interest rate policy we adopt. If British interest rates fall below the levels in other countries, then obviously people will not want to hold their wealth in sterling and the currency will tend to fall in value.

One could of course argue that that is just what is wanted, in order to reduce the price of our goods abroad and thus to improve our competitiveness. But this is a dangerous route to go down. It runs the risk of a major increase in inflation at home, as import prices rise. This is why we have chosen to rely on extra government spending and lower taxes as the engines of recovery, rather than on a depreciation of the currency.

So how can such a depreciation be avoided? Experience has

shown that the exchange rate can always be maintained if interest rates are kept high enough. The key question is, How high would they need to go? For this purpose we should focus mainly on real interest rates, since these are what affect business investment. If our policy would raise real interest rates sky-high, it might kill off as many jobs as it created, leaving us no better off than before.

To investigate this issue we need to ask three questions. First, how will our policies affect the public debt, and second how does the public debt affect interest rates. The third question relates to the balance of trade.

THE PUBLIC DEBT

Will our policies lead to a rapid accumulation of public debt? The question is important because if debt accumulated too much, doubts would arise as to whether we could ultimately pay the interest on the debt. So in measuring the size of the debt we should measure it relative to the tax base out of which the interest has to be paid—in other words we measure it relative to national income.

Judged by this standard, the debt is now unusually low. In fact it is a good deal lower than it has been for most of the last two hundred years (Fig. 28). And how would it evolve under our policies? On *present* policies the debt is set to fall for the rest of the decade. This is a truly amazing situation. For nearly all economists of whatever persuasion (from monetarist Chicago to Keynesian Cambridge) would agree that in a slump the debt/income ratio should be allowed to rise (unless it is already unacceptably high, which it is not).

So what room for manœuvre have we? We can start by asking what level of public borrowing would be consistent with a constant debt/income ratio. For this ratio to be constant, the debt would have to grow as fast as money income (say, 9 per cent per annum). Now the existing debt is £170 billion and the change in the debt is the same as public borrowing.[4] So public borrowing could be 9 per cent of £170 billion, or about £15 billion. This compares with £7 billion planned for 1986–7.

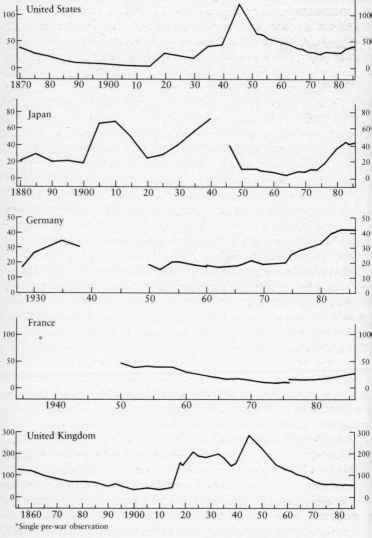

Fig. 28. Historical Public Debt/GNP Ratios for Five Major OECD Countries

So even without an increase in the debt/income ratio, there is room for manœuvre. On top of this, a moderate rise in the debt/income ratio is perfectly acceptable in a slump.

Suppose we embarked on a policy which increased the debt/income ratio. Would it then go on rising for ever?[5] No. There are three possible fail–safe mechanisms. First, the aim of our policy is to restore vitality to the economy. Thus once the gloom and doom has been dispersed, we would expect a revival of private spending propensities. This would enable us to reduce the degree of budgetary injection and thus stop the debt/income ratio rising any further. Second, it is unlikely that world real interest rates will stay as high as now indefinitely. If they fall, it would be much easier to hold the debt/income ratio, because the lower interest rates would stimulate private spending and also cut the burden of interest payments on the public debt. Third, the debt/income ratio is in any case self-limiting. It will not go on rising for ever. You can take this on trust or read the next two paragraphs.

The real deficit can be divided into two parts: real interest payments and the primary deficit. If the primary deficit is constant and the real debt is rising, the ratio of the primary deficit to the debt will fall steadily. Thus the rate of growth of the debt will fall steadily, until it eventually becomes no greater than the growth of real income.

Equilibrium will be reached when both debt and real income are growing at the same rate, or

$$\frac{Real\ deficit}{Real\ debt} + Real\ interest\ rate = Real\ growth\ rate.$$

Thus, whatever the real deficit, the debt/income ratio will be self-limiting, subject to one condition: that the real growth rate of the economy be greater than the real rate of interest. This condition has nearly always been satisfied, and is likely to be satisfied in the future, even if it is not now. World real interest rates are now unusually high, and are most unlikely to be as high over any longish time period.(Sudden spikes are not important for this particular analysis). Moreover, British interest rates are unlikely to rise much relative to world rates if our policies are followed, since the debt/income ratio of other countries is currently rising rapidly, while ours is not (see Fig. 28).

So our policies would not lead to an ever-exploding debt. They might however lead to a period in which the debt/income ratio was rising somewhat. How much does this matter? Does it mean that real interest rates would be much higher than they would otherwise be, and in this way crowd out at least part of the budgetary stimulus?

THE EFFECT OF THE DEBT ON INTEREST RATES

It is easy to see why this might happen if our economy were isolated from the rest of the world. For if the government tried to borrow more, people might easily say 'If they want us to lend more, they will have to give us a higher real rate of return'.

But in an open economy with rapid electronic transfer of funds and information, things are bound to be different. On a typical day now, something like $200 billion-worth of funds are switched from bonds of one currency into bonds of another.[6] Exchange controls inhibiting this flow have been progressively dismantled and in Britain they disappeared in 1979.[7] There is thus an integrated world capital market, in which investors are constantly comparing the returns on bonds in different currencies and choosing portfolios to maximize their advantage. In this huge market the stall marked 'British government debt' is a fairly small one. So what happens when the stall marked 'British government debt' starts selling more?

It is helpful to think of British real interest rates as being equal to world real interest rates plus a 'differential'

British interest rate − Expected British inflation
= US interest rate − Expected US inflation.

When more British debt is sold, the total of world debt changes by such a tiny proportion that world interest rates change to a negligible extent. So the key question is, What happens to the differential?

To get started, let us see why one might, as a first approximation, expect real interest rates to be the same in all countries. Take Britain and the US as an example, and suppose investors are seeking the highest expected return for their money. Then they will put all their money into one or other currency unless the returns they expect are the same in both currencies. Since prices adjust to clear the market, it must happen that all of both currencies get held, and therefore the expected return must have been equalized. Looking at the matter from the US point of view, this means that US interest rates must equal British interest rates minus the expected fall in the pound.[8] The same is true from the point of view of the British investor. Thus

British interest rate − Expected fall in the pound
$$= US \; interest \; rate.$$

So the next question is how people form their expectations about exchange rate changes. In the very long run exchange rates have to adjust to differences in inflation rates, otherwise competitiveness would go on changing for ever. So in the long run

Expected fall in the pound
$$= Expected \; British \; inflation − Expected \; US \; inflation.$$

Suppose that such a relationship also held in the short run. We can now combine it with our first relation and discover what we were looking for; namely that

British interest rate − Expected British inflation
$$= US \; interest \; rate − Expected \; US \; inflation.$$

So real interest rates are equalized.

In fact this will not happen, for a number of reasons. First, exchange rate expectations are not entirely based on expected inflation differentials. They also depend on whether the exchange rate is floating or (temporarily) fixed, and on how far the exchange rate is out of line.[9]

These are factors which would prevent the equalization of real exchange rates except in the long run. But for our purpose the important issue is a second question: Is there a 'risk premium' which would lead to permanent real interest differentials, and in particular does this differential rise with increases in the British debt?

This is an empirical question. Academic studies do not give an unambiguous answer, but one can say that no clear evidence exists that past increases in British debt have induced rises in British real interest rates (other things equal). To give the flavour of this, we can look at some simple relationships (not adjusted for any other factors).

In Figure 29 we plot the ratio of public debt to GDP against the real interest differential. There is no relation at all. It is

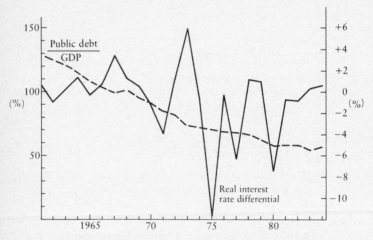

Fig. 29. UK Public Debt/GDP Ratio and Real Interest Rate Differentials, 1961–84.

especially interesting that the huge British post-war debt had so little effect on the interest differential (the excess of British rates over other OECD rates). In Figure 30 we plot British public debt relative to world public debt against the real interest differential. Again there is no effect. One could of course argue that it is the flows of new debt which matter, but I can assure you that there is also no relation between the real deficit/GDP ratio and real interest differentials (or between it and real interest rates).[10]

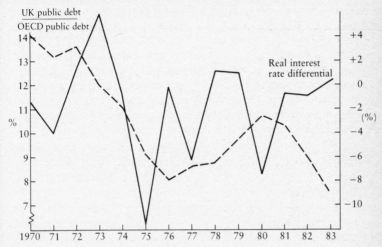

Fig. 30. UK Share of OECD Public Debt and Real Interest Rate Differentials, 1970–83.

THE TRADE BALANCE

Finally, we need to refer to the problem of the trade balance. If we expanded our economy while holding the exchange rate fixed, our trade balance would worsen. Eventually, to restore it, competitiveness would have to be improved by a fall in the value of the pound.[11] If the fall is not to occur now, holders of sterling have to be compensated for the future fall by receiving a higher real interest rate. This is true, but the magnitude of the effect is not likely to be great. For suppose pessimistically that we needed ultimately to depreciate by 5 per cent more than otherwise (a large amount to result from a policy change).[12] This would require a 1 per cent higher interest rate than otherwise for five years. Since at the same time our public debt would be falling relative to that of other countries, it does not seem too much of a risk.

We should certainly not expect that real interest rates would rise substantially. Moreover, the USA has done well despite high interest rates. So the notion that high interest rates could abort the recovery is absurd.

EMS MEMBERSHIP

In any case, there is one further weapon besides interest rates on which we could rely for the short-run defence of the exchange rate. This is the European Monetary System (EMS). This is a system of semi-fixed exchange rates including all the main EEC countries (except at present Britain). A country's currency has a par value against the other currencies, and if its actual value gets out of line by more than a small amount, the country is obliged to take action. It can either intervene in the foreign exchange market (buying or selling its currency), or it can raise or lower short-term interest rates, or it can do something more drastic. All these options are of course available even without being in the EMS, and we could always announce an exchange rate target without joining. But there are two specific advantages of EMS membership. First an EMS exchange rate is a much more definite commitment than an 'exchange rate target'. It runs more chance of cutting out destabilizing speculation, even though it still has to be defended by the standard tools. Second, the other EMS Central Banks stand ready to lend to a currency that is in trouble, which again helps to damp down destabilizing speculation.

It would not of course be necessary to enter the EMS at exactly the existing parity. In fact, one advantage of joining is that we could opt for a once-and-for-all gain in competitiveness without this setting up the same inflationary expectations as if competitiveness improves from a market-driven depreciation of the exchange rate.[13]

So our policies are workable. They will increase jobs and they need not lead to higher inflation or soaring real interest rates.

Summary

1. It is not true that extra spending cannot create jobs because of its effects on price inflation and on interest rates.
2. Extra spending creates jobs because prices are sticky.
3. To ensure that inflation does not increase we need not only to contain wages but also to prevent the value of the pound from falling.
4. This can be done by holding interest rates high enough. For this reason we have to rely on the budget rather than lower interest rates as the main domestic engine of expansion.
5. There is no reason why our real interest rates need rise much relative to world real interest rates. By historical standards, our public debt is low relative to national income, and it is also falling relative to the debt of the OECD governments.
6. Our debt/income ratio could be allowed to rise a little for a few years to help us overcome a severe depression.
7. To help stabilize the value of the pound against short-run speculative attacks, Britain should join the European Monetary System.

12

Alternative Policies: No to Work-Sharing and Early Retirement

The person-in-the-street's favourite remedy for unemployment is work-sharing. But this idea is fundamentally misconceived, because it is based on the wrong theory of unemployment (or no theory at all).

The argument starts with the 'lump of output' fallacy. It assumes that the amount of output to be produced is somehow given. The reason could be that we do not need any more output, which, as I have said, is an immoral view. Or it could be that there is some physical limit to what we can produce (for example, due to shortage of capital). Or it could be that the government is simply not willing to let more output be demanded.

If output is given, the question becomes: 'What is the most humane way of producing it?' Obviously, we should let everybody who wants work do some of it. So if the output requires 1 billion person-hours a week and there are 25 million people, let them all work 40 hours a week. This would be better than having, say, a 44-hour week and 10 per cent unemployment.

If output *were* given, this argument would be absolutely right. But output is not given. Output is only limited to the extent that, if we reduce unemployment, inflation will increase more than otherwise.

But if inflation depends only on unemployment, then any action that cuts unemployment will add to inflationary pressure. If we are willing to accept more inflationary pressure, we can cut unemployment in two ways:

(i) Keep output constant but reduce hours per worker, thus increasing employment.

(ii) Increase output and employment (with hours per worker constant), by expanding the demand for output.

Clearly, the second of these is better since it alone expands both employment *and* output.

Now take a more cautious position. Suppose we are not willing to accept increased inflationary pressure. Is there any mileage to be got from work-sharing? Alas, none. For it will only increase inflationary pressure. This will lead the government to reduce the demand for output. Thus output will end up lower than before, and unemployment the same. The whole thought-experiment which depended on constant output, will turn out to have been built on shifting sands.

The problem with those who advocate work-sharing is that they do not have any clear theory of what is limiting output. Satiation is not a plausible theory. Capital does not pose an absolute limit. The only plausible theory of why output is low is because governments are afraid of the inflationary consequences of expansion.

My argument assumes that work-sharing does not affect the NAIRU. Is there any reason why it should? As we have seen, for inflation to be stable, unemployment has to be such that firms and unions are willing to settle at the prevailing rate of settlements and not try running ahead. Does the level of hours per worker affect what that critical level of unemployment is? The evidence shows that changes in hours do *nothing* to alter the critical level of unemployment.[1]

We have not so far discussed the question of what happens to workers' weekly real income when their hours are cut by work-sharing. Implicitly, we have been assuming that it falls, with real hourly pay remaining constant. This is what has happened voluntarily in Holland. But in Britain it seems likely that workers would in fact resist this cut in weekly earnings.[2] But if weekly earnings are maintained, costs per unit of output, and thus prices, have to rise. So the feasible real weekly wage falls, and this tends to increase unemployment as was shown in Figure 13(a). This must follow if weekly wages are what workers care about when they bargain.

The government could, of course, offset this tendency by making up the income difference (or part of it), when workers' incomes are cut by falling hours. This was the essence of the

Temporary Short-Time Working Compensation Scheme, which was used to encourage work-sharing rather than redundancies in the late 1970s and early 1980s. But one is bound to ask whether the money would not have been better spent on stimulating demand rather than on subsidizing jobs (that eventually disappear anyway) in the declining industries.

Having said all this against it,[3] let's make some positive points. Manual workers' hours of work have been coming down since the nineteenth century (for men from, say, 60 a week at the turn of the century to 44 today). This is the absolutely appropriate reaction to higher real wages—people choose voluntarily to have more leisure and not only to have more goods. This tendency should continue in future. But it should not be accelerated as a panic reaction to unemployment. Above all, people should not be forced to work shorter hours than they want, or made to feel bad because they are doing overtime. Britain has since 1975 reduced hours worked more than any other major country,[4] and in fact the countries which have reduced their hours least have had the smallest rise in unemployment (Japan and the United States).

EARLY RETIREMENT

The same principles apply to early retirement. The alternatives for reducing unemployment are now

(i) Keep output and employment constant, but get some older people to retire, thus reducing unemployment.

(ii) Increase output by increasing employment.

Both are equally inflationary. But once again the second option is clearly preferable. Early retirement will not reduce the NAIRU.

Of course as living standards have risen, people have tended to retire earlier (though again, the trend is much less in the US and Japan).[5] This is fine, but nobody should be made to feel bad because they have not retired and given their job to a younger man. If the government bribes people to retire early (as under the Job Release Scheme),[6] this is a relatively cheap way of reducing unemployment. But compared with the Community Programme, it does nothing to increase the amount of useful work being done in the community.

PART-TIME EMPLOYMENT

There is one further issue. If people cannot get full-time jobs, why not make it more worth their while to get part-time jobs? At present someone on Unemployment Benefit can work part-time and get benefit for the other days, provided he would normally work on the other days and is willing to work on them. If he is on Supplementary Benefit, a similar split is possible. The person's income will be made up to the Supplementary Benefit level if he is working part time and his part-time earnings fall below the Supplementary Benefit level.[7] But once again he must be willing to work on the other days.

Should part-time employment be made more advantageous, with no requirement of willingness to work on the other days? It is not obvious. We do not want it to be too attractive for people to establish themselves in part-time work—on benefits paid by others. Of course, we welcome the growth of part-time female employment; that reflects a flexible labour market. But for me to work part time and have my income topped up for the rest of the week out of other people's pockets is a different issue altogether. It is not an efficient arrangement, and not one that requires any further encouragement. If people want full-time incomes, we want them to be in full-time work. If they stop looking for this (and thus stop reducing inflationary pressure), full-time work will never come back.

To assume that we cannot have more full-time work is a counsel of despair. We should never accept it. This book has aimed to show that we can get more jobs. Our present recession is largely man-made (by people living not a million miles away). It is within our power to reverse it. Only that way can we bring justice to the unemployed and prosperity to all.

Summary

1. The argument for work-sharing and for early retirement is that output is fixed. If it were, it would be good to share the work around and give it to younger people.
2. But output is not fixed. It is limited by the NAIRU. If unemployment falls for whatever reason, inflation will increase. This is so whether unemployment is reduced by work-sharing, early retirement, or by increases in output. Of these, more output is much the best.
3. But if inflation is to be held stable, neither work-sharing nor early retirement will reduce unemployment.
4. Reductions in hours will be particularly unsuccessful if workers try to maintain the same real weekly income while working shorter hours. This is bound to increase the NAIRU.

Further Reading

I have tried to write this book in a way that makes sense to non-economists. For those who need a more basic introduction I suggest D. Begg, R. Dornbusch, and S. Fischer, *Economics* (which includes British data) or, at a slightly more advanced level, R. Dornbusch and S. Fischer, *Macroeconomics*.

The chief source of information about British unemployment is the Department of Employment *Gazette*. The Manpower Services Commission (Moorfoot, Sheffield, S1 4PQ) produce an excellent *Quarterly Report*. The Charter for Jobs (Suite 107, Southbank House, Black Prince Road, London SE1 7SJ) produce a useful monthly *Economic Report*, and the Employment Institute (at the same address) produces a series of pamphlets about basic unemployment issues.

At a more technical level, much of the material in this book is explained more fully in the following places:

(i) Causes of unemployment:
   Layard, P. R. G. and Nickell, S. J. (1986), 'Unemployment in Britain', *Economica*, Supplement.
   Layard, P. R. G. and Nickell, S. J., 'The Performance of the British Labour Market', London School of Economics, *Mimeo*, May 1986.

(ii) Policies on the NAIRU:
   Johnson, G. E., and Layard, P. R. G. (1986), 'The Natural Rate of Unemployment and Labour Market Policy', in O. Ashenfelter and P. R. G. Layard (eds.), *Handbook of Labour Economics*, North Holland.
   Jackman, R. A., Layard, P. R. G., and Pissarides, C. (1986), 'Policies for Reducing the Natural Rate of Unemployment', in J. L. Butkiewicz, K. J. Koford and J. B. Miller (eds.), *Keynes' Economic Legacy*, Praeger.

(iii) Incomes policy:
   Layard, P. R. G. (1982), *More Jobs Less Inflation*, Grant MacIntyre.

(iv) Fiscal and monetary policy:

Blanchard, O., Dornbusch, R., and Layard, P. R. G. (1986), *Restoring Europe's Prosperity*, Centre for European Policy Studies, Brussels, especially chapter on 'Europe: The Case for Unsustainable Growth'.

I apologize for the way in which the book pays more attention to male than female unemployment. The reason is only that the evidence is so much more straightforward. Someone with time to interpret the data should write a book with the opposite emphasis.

Notes

CHAPTER 1 The argument

1. Department of Employment, *Gazette*, March 1981, Table 5.6, and Department of Employment, *Gazette*, August 1979, Table 125. Data relate to hourly earnings excluding overtime.

CHAPTER 2 The basic facts about unemployment

1. The unemployment rate of the insured population was higher than now, but the unemployment rate of the uninsured population was much lower than that of the insured population.
2. Metcalf, Nickell, and Floros (1982).
3. OECD (1982)
4. National Labour Market Board, Unemployment Insurance Division, Sweden (1984).
5. All figures from OPCS, *Labour Force Survey*. For 1984 (unpublished figures) we have distributed across reasons for unemployment those who lost their job over three years ago in proportion to all other unemployed people who had ever worked.
6. OPCS, *General Household Survey* 1983, Table 7.28. All data are for males. Unemployment rates are unemployed as a percentage of total labour force (including self-employed).
7. Micklewright (1983).
8. OECD, *Economic Outlook*, June 1985, Tables 13 and 15. In Germany, under 25s have 10.1 per cent unemployment, compared with 8.3 per cent overall (September 1984).
9. Layard in Freeman and Wise (1978); Wells (1983).
10. OPCS, *General Household Survey* 1983, Table 7.24.
11. OECD, *Employment Outlook*, September 1985,Table B.
12. Against this must be set an increase of some $\frac{3}{4}$ million in the self-employed. (Department of Employment, *Gazette*, Table 1.1.)
13. This is the key fact, though it is also true that the high unemployment areas have had a lower proportionate rise in unemployment

than more favoured regions. For example, consider the figures in Table 16.

Table 16. Changes in Unemployment in Northern England and South-East England, 1979–85

	Unemployment rates (%)	
	North	South-East
1979	7.3	3.0
1985	18.2	9.8
Absolute increase 1979–85	10.9	6.8
Proportional increase 1979–85	149.0	227.0

14. Department of Employment, *Gazette*, November 1985, Table 2.4.
15. Moylan, Millar, and Davies (1984), p. 30. Industry is defined by SIC two-digit category.
16. Construction has always had much the highest unemployment rate but in the 1970s manufacturing had below the national average.

CHAPTER 3 **The inflation/unemployment quandary**

1. This is based on the following crude equation (1955–85)

$$\dot{p} - \dot{p}_{-1} = 3.6 - 7.7 \log U + 0.48 \, T - 13.0 \, I$$
$$(t = 2.9) \qquad (t = 2.4) \qquad (t = 4.1)$$

$\bar{R}^2 = 0.47$, $DW = 2.02$,

where $\dot{p}$ is the percentage increase in the GDP deflator at factor cost over the previous year (see Fig. 11),

$\dot{p}_{-1}$ is the comparable inflation rate for the previous year,

U is the percentage unemployment rate (OECD standardized rate),

T is date minus 1954, and

I is an incomes policy dummy for 1976.

The implied NAIRU for 1986 is 11.7, obtained by solving the following equation for U:

$$0 = 3.6 - 7.7 \log U + 0.48 \, (1986 - 1954).$$

This rate is an OECD standardized rate and is therefore about 0.5 points above the comparable official rate.

The equation also says that at 10 per cent unemployment, a 1 per cent decrease in unemployment would increase inflation by 0.77 percentage points. A rough figure of unity is assumed in the diagram.

For a more sophisticated analysis see Layard and Nickell (1986), who estimate the male NAIRU for 1980–3 at 10.5 but rising somewhat.

The diagram in Figure 11 is not tautological, for unless the theory were approximately true, there could be no simple expression for the NAIRU such that (U − NAIRU) was related to $\dot{p} - \dot{p}_{-1}$.

2. Layard and Nickell (1986), Table 15 suggests that a demand shock that led to an additional 0.4 percentage point-years of unemployment would raise inflation by 0.6 percentage points, i.e. inflation would rise by $1\frac{1}{2}$ per cent a year if unemployment was 1 percentage point lower. Grubb, Jackman, and Layard (1982) Table VII, using a very different model, get a very similar estimate (of 1.4). See also the recent mimeo by Layard and Nickell listed on p. 161, which presents a more complete analysis.

3. Layard and Nickell (1986). In that paper the distinction between changes in the NAIRU and 'overkill' is drawn very sharply. In Chapter 4 below we allow for more interaction between demand shocks and the short-run NAIRU.

4. Clearly the feasible real wage will be affected by the degree of monopoly in product markets and many other variables discussed below. It is not a technological datum. It may also rise somewhat with unemployment, as price mark-ups are reduced. But this does not affect the basic argument.

5. This is so unless the prices of things produced have risen by the same amount, i.e. there is no change in the terms of trade. If p is log prices, w log wages, and p^* log import prices

$$p = aw + (1-a) \, p^* + \text{constant}.$$
$$w - p = \left[\frac{1-a}{a}\right] (p - p^*) + \text{constant}.$$

6. Thus the government could quite well use the revenue from the higher prices to maintain real wages (by cutting indirect or direct taxes).

7. If we take the ratio of the International Monetary Fund commodity price index to the unit value index for exports of industrial countries, this stood in 1980 at unity—lower than in any of the previous 25 years (except for 1971 and 1975 which were very slightly lower). By 1985(III) the ratio had fallen to 0.79.

8. If t_1 are employers' tax rates, t_2 direct tax rates, t_3 indirect tax rates, p log prices, w log wages, and there are no imported materials, then

$$p = t_3 + w + t_1 + \text{constant},$$

and

$$w - t_2 - p = \text{constant} - (t_1 + t_2 + t_3).$$

The left-hand side measures real take-home pay.

CHAPTER 4   The supply side

1. For a fuller discussion of this see Jackman, Layard, and Pissarides (1985), which also shows employers' estimates of labour shortage. These closely corroborate the vacancy series.

2. The family may also be eligible for Housing Benefit, though traditionally this has been less than the 100 per cent of housing costs covered by Supplementary Benefit.

3. Under the new Social Security Act only 80 per cent of rates are now paid.

4. Taking all the unemployed, the proportions receiving benefit are as shown in Table 17.

Table 17.   *Proportion of Unemployed Receiving Benefits, 1984, by Type of Benefit (percentages)*

	Men	Women	Total
Unemployment Benefit only	19	33	23
Unemployment Benefit and Supplementary Benefit	8	3	7
Supplementary Benefit only	62	44	56
None	11	20	14
Total	100	100	100

Figures relate to November 1984 and are from Department of Health and Social Security, *Unemployment Benefit Statistics*, 1985, Table 1. In 1971 the proportions (for all registered unemployed men and women) were: Unemployment Benefit only—41 per cent; Unemployment Benefit and Supplementary Benefit—12 per cent; Supplementary Benefit only—26 per cent; no benefit—21 per cent.

5. *General Household Survey*, 1983, Table 7.8 (An additional 4 per cent were reported to be unemployed.)

6. (i) In this calculation housing costs are included in incomes while unemployed and when in work. (ii) The calculation relates to the position in the first few months of unemployment. But in fact the ratio is very much the same, however long the person has been out of work (Dilnot and Morris, 1984).

7. Atkinson and Micklewright (1982).

8. In Layard and Nickell (1986) this approach is used, and the result is an overall elasticity of unemployment with respect to the replacement ratio of about 0.7 at the sample mean. By contrast Minford (1985, p. 20) gets an elasticity of about $2\frac{1}{2}$. This must be because his real wage equation does not include any productivity-related variable, and real benefits therefore emerge with a very big effect. Contrary to his view (pp. 27–8), there is no problem of including productivity-related variables, since these, though endogenous, can be instrumented. Doing so does not materially affect our results. Minford says (p. 27) that including productivity-like terms does not affect his results, but this only raises further questions about what is going on in his real wage equation.

9. Narendranathan, Nickell, and Stern (1985). This measures the leftwards shift of the supply curve for labour and is thus an upper bound on the shift in total employment. Minford's measure of the leftwards shift of the supply curve involves an elasticity of 10, compared with 0.5 in the work quoted here. For a criticism see previous footnote.

10. Clearly it is difficult to check whether somebody fails to avail of work opportunities that exist. In the US the test relates to job search. Unemployment Insurance recipients have to make a certain number of applications to employers each week. Random audit exercises have been able to disqualify up to 20 per cent of recipients, simply by checking whether the claimed applications were actually made.

11. Department of Employment and Department of Health and Social Security (1981). For other evidence on the proportion of the unem-

ployed either working or not seeking work see Department of Employment, *Gazette*, October 1985, p. 393. Note that the black economy (i.e. paid work not disclosed to the Inland Revenue or Department of Health and Social Security) mainly consists of second jobs by people already employed (Pahl 1984).

12. The sources for the last two paragraphs, respectively, are Budd, Levine, and Smith (1985), and Layard and Nickell (1986).

13. In Layard and Nickell (1986) we were unable to find such an effect, but Blanchard and Summers (1986) find it, especially in France and Germany. In an extreme view the NAIRU depends only on recent unemployment. In this case the NAIRU could in principle be anything, depending on past history. This is a case of pure 'hysteresis' (see p. 63). It could arise if, for example, wages were set by unions, and unions cared only about people employed in the recent past, i.e. they only cared for 'insiders' and not for 'outsiders' (see below).

14. Partial hysteresis can be represented in the following simplified way.

$$\dot{p} - \dot{p}_{-1} = -aU + bU_{-1} + c, \qquad\qquad (a > b).$$

The long-run NAIRU is $U^* = c/(a-b)$. The short-run NAIRU is $U_s^* = (c+bU_{-1})/a$. If $U_{-1} > U^*$, then $U_{-1} > U_s^* > U^*$. So unemployment can only be reduced slowly without increasing inflation.

With full hysteresis there is no long-run NAIRU but lower unemployment means a higher level of inflation. We have

$$\dot{p} - \dot{p}_{-1} = -a(U - U_{-1}) + c,$$

which implies (by integration)

$$\dot{p} = -aU + cT + \text{constant}.$$

This is the 'old-style' Phillips curve with drift added in.

15. The total demand for labour is $N + V$ (employed + vacancies). Since the unemployment rate has risen, N/L has fallen; and, since the vacancy rate has fallen, V/N has fallen (and thus so has V/L). Hence $(N + V)/L$ has fallen.

16. Suppose unemployment doubled with the same structure, i.e. 80 skilled and 320 unskilled. The index would still be the same. This is what we want because we are looking for an index of what could have caused the unemployment to increase. Of course, if we asked how many people were structurally unemployed, it would be twice as many in the second case as in the first.

17. One dimension that cannot easily be studied formally is mismatch by sex. In so far as jobs tend to be male- or female-intensive, there may well have been a disproportionate growth in female-intensive vacancies.

18. Jackman, Layard, and Pissarides (1985).

19. Daniel and Stigloe (1978), and Confederation of British Industry (1984). The Confederation of British Industry commissioned Gallup to conduct a survey to which about 800 firms replied (accounting for about 4 million employees). They were asked what effect various possible changes might have on the number of employees in their organization. The replies were as shown in Table 18.

Table 18.   *Industrialists' Assessment of Effect of Policy Changes on Employment (percentage response)*

	Definitely increase employment	Possibly increase employment	Make no difference	Decrease employment	Don't know
Abolition or reduction in redundancy entitlements	5	14	75	3	4
Abolition or reduction in unfair dismissal rights	3	7	12	1	77
Reduce collective rights of unions	5	17	67	5	6
Reduction in pay and fringe benefits	9	37	45	4	6

By contrast, the Wilson Committee (1980) did report employment protection as an often-cited deterrent to investment.

20. This is not because the jobs available are bad jobs. There are practically no vacancies for low-level jobs.

21. Johnson and Layard (1986), Table 6.5.

22. See note 13.

CHAPTER 5   Aggregate demand

1. It might be argued that the calculation of potential output should be explicitly related to the calculation of the NAIRU. But given the

effect of recent actual output on the NAIRU, we have drawn potential output here as a trend.

2. This is because total 'final demand' is the first three items plus exports, but imports meet some of the demand, so that domestic product only has to satisfy final demand minus imports.

3. As regards measurement, Non-oil income at market prices is computed as [(GDP at factor cost − North Sea oil profits) × (GDP at market prices/GDP at factor cost)]. The tax rate on non-oil income equals (Total taxes on income − Petroleum Revenue Tax − Corporation Tax on North Sea oil profits)/Non-oil income at market prices + All other taxes/GDP at market prices.

   As regards the theoretical analysis of fiscal stance, North Sea oil complicates the analysis considerably. It is however wrong to suggest that North Sea oil taxes should not be counted as taxes because North Sea oil profits after tax generate little spending. If this is so, there is a need for other spending to compensate. It is not clear whether full employment would require a higher or lower budget deficit in the presence or absence of North Sea oil.

4. Suppose we adopt the simplest Keynesian model

$$Y = cY(1-t) + G + I + NX,$$

where Y is real output, t the average tax rate (i.e. share of taxes in GDP), G is real transfers (all spent) *plus* real public expenditure on goods and services, I is real investment, and NX is net exports. Let Y^* indicate full employment output. Thus

$$\frac{Y}{Y^*} = \frac{1}{1 - c(1-t)} \left(\frac{G}{Y^*} + \frac{I}{Y^*} + \frac{NX}{Y^*} \right).$$

In other words, the rate of unemployment depends on the ratio of taxes to actual GNP and the ratio of G, I, and NX to potential GNP.

5. They can now be inferred by comparing the interest rate on indexed and unindexed government bonds, after suitable allowance for taxes and uncertainty.

6. This story emerges from any index. The index given here shows relative unit normal labour costs. This is to avoid the problem that the prices of goods traded underweight the most rapidly rising prices precisely because these lead to lower trade.

7. Forsyth and Kay (1980) present the strongest argument in favour of this view. For a discussion, see Buiter and Miller (1983).

8. For changes in the adjusted deficit, 1979–84, see Layard *et al.*

(1984). 1985 adjusted deficit = 1984 adjusted deficit + change in actual deficit. (OECD, *Economic Outlook*, June 1985, Table 3). The unemployment rates are OECD standardized rates (see sources to Fig. 3).

9. This has worked in three ways. First, open-ended benefits have allowed long-term unemployment to persist here, while in the US poverty has forced people back to work (real wages have barely grown for a decade). Second, there is no employment protection in the US; 'hire and fire' in the US has always led to greater employment fluctuations there. Third, the trade unions have been in decline in the US for 15 years, while in Europe they were on the rise throughout the 1970s.

10. Suppose pricing is as follows:

$$p = aw + (1-a)p^* + \text{constant} \qquad (a < 1),$$

or

$$w - p = (p-p^*)(1-a)/a + \text{constant},$$

where p is log prices, w log wages and p^* log world prices. Suppose wage setting is as follows:

$$w - p = b - cU + \text{constant},$$

where U is unemployment. Hence the supply side of the economy is

$$U = b/c - (p-p^*)(1-a)/ac + \text{constant}. \qquad (1)$$

Suppose also that trade balance requires higher unemployment (to restrain imports) if our relative prices rise. Thus

$$U = d(p-p^*) + \text{constant}. \qquad (2)$$

It follows from (1) and (2) that $(p-p^*)$ is an increasing function of the wage-push parameter b, and so is $w-p$.

CHAPTER 6   Alternative theories

1. Layard and Nickell (1986). This is holding capital constant. Nickell and I give evidence that if $N/K = f(W/P, A)$ where N/K is labour/capital, W/P is real labour cost and A an index of output per unit of input, $f_2 \simeq 0$. So A does not affect the relation of W/P and N/K. Going on, A must raise output. But MP_N (= W/P) is constant, so MP_K must rise for given N, K (by Euler's theorem). Thus technical

progress is labour saving (MP_K/MP_N up at a given N/K).

2. In October 1978, there were 5.1 million manual workers in manufacturing (Department of Employment, *Gazette*, December 1978, p. 138), working, on average, 42.8 hours per week (*Gazette*, Table 5.6), giving a total of 220 million hours per week. Bosworth and Dawkins (1980, Table 4), show that of these, 38.8 million hours per week were worked outside the hours 8 a.m.–6 p.m.—14 per cent of the total.

CHAPTER 7   Cutting unemployment with both blades

1. HM Treasury (1985).
2. See Davies and Metcalf (1985). For up-to-date evidence on the cost per job of different policies as estimated on the Treasury model, see the very useful Ready Reckoner obtainable from Christopher Barclay at the House of Commons Library. Corresponding analysis using the National Institute's model appears in *National Institute Economic Review*, February 1986.
3. Between 1979 and 1984, the number of employees dropped by 1,990,000, of which government and local authorities 130,000, public corporations 345,000, and private sector 1,515,000 (CSO, *Economic Trends*, March 1985). Public corporations are those defined that way in 1979.
4. Suppose aggregate demand is given by

$$Y = C(Y,t) + I(r) + G + NX(e,Y). \tag{1}$$

where Y is real output, r real interest rates, G government spending on goods and services, t tax rates, and e is the exchange rate. If e is held constant and r has to be held at the world level (or even raised somewhat), then the only engines of recovery are G and t.

Suppose for simplicity there is perfect capital mobility with international interest rates equal to r^*. The demand for money is given by

$$\frac{M}{P} = L(Y,r). \tag{2}$$

This is the basic Mundell–Fleming model. If we now increase M/P on its own, this increases Y, from (2). Using (1), we can compute how much e must have depreciated. If we increase G on its own, Y

will not change because the appreciation of *e* will offset it. Hence by a balanced increase in *G* and *M/P* we can get an increase in *Y* with no change in *e* (two instruments, two targets).

CHAPTER 8 A new deal for the long-term unemployed

1. This is based on Layard, Metcalf, and O'Brien (1986), which benefited greatly from talks with John Cahill and Liz Hartley-Brewer. The same approach was advocated by the House of Commons Employment Committee (1986).
2. Department of Employment, *Gazette*, Table 2.6 gives the flow into LTU and the stock. Outflow = Inflow − Changes in stock.
3. Department of Employment, *Gazette*, Table 2.6.
4. NEDO (1985).
5. Confederation of British Industry, *Cutting Unemployment Now: The Opportunity for the 1986 Budget*, November 1985.
6. One can computer mechanically the implied marginal wage elasticity. This is percentage change in employment/percentage change in wage = 2/25 = 0.08. The wage effect will be strongest in the more competitive sectors, i.e. export sectors or small enterprises like retail, catering, hotels, repairs, and cleaning. For an earlier discussion of a rather different scheme, using very conservative parameters, see Layard and Nickell (1980).
7. Average duration = Stock/Flow = 1.6/1.0. The average remaining expected duration rises somewhat with duration.
8. The total outflow is 1 million, but Department of Employment information indicates that only one half of these enter employment. Some of these people would in fact enter the public sector, and others would enter contracting firms not eligible for subsidy.
9. If the employers insisted, the workers would have to be on one-year contracts. Employers would have to have the right to select individual workers and to fire them if they did not perform.
10. National Labour Market Board (1984).
11. Beveridge (1942), pp. 11, 128.
12. Beveridge (1942), p. 163. However, he doubted whether the condition of attendance at a work or training centre was practicable if it had to be applied to men by the millions or the hundred thousands. That is why our proposal is for a more substantial form of work than attendance at a centre.
13. Narendranathan, Nickell, and Stern (1985).
14. Dilnot, Kay, and Morris (1984). The Fowler proposals have the

major disadvantage of giving all means-tested family support to the husband.

15. Treasury and Civil Service Committee (1983).

CHAPTER 9　Targeting the jobs and upgrading the workers

1. This section is based on Jackman, Layard, and Metcalf (1985).
2. Department of Employment, *New Earnings Survey*, and Thatcher (1968).
3. On elasticities see, for example, Nissim (1984).
4. Department of Employment, *Gazette*, May 1978. This result was found both by questionnaire surveys and using econometric methods with a control group that was not eligible for the subsidy because it was in the wrong area. Clearly some substitution of employment between areas may have occurred which is not captured in the 40 per cent estimate I have quoted.
5. There is evidence that in a steady state, the sum of gross increases in employment at the level of the establishment equals 3 per cent of total employment. If we allow for maximum growth in aggregate employment, we could then assume that say 6 per cent of employees would be subsidized. Since one-third of employees are in 'assisted' areas we should be subsidizing 2 per cent of employment. Total employers' National Insurance contributions are approximately £12 billion. The cost is 2 per cent of this. If the subsidy covers all increases over 90 per cent of last year, this figure will be increased by a multiple of $(6 + 10)/6$.
6. Prais and Wagner (1985). This is based on the International Education Association study of advancement in mathematics conducted in 1963/4. But subsequent evidence quoted by the authors confirms the general impression.
7. Department of Education and Science, *Statistical Bulletin*, 5/82 March 1982, Table 16. The figures of teachers' qualifications are not quite so bad when related to the hours of mathematics teaching, since those qualified in maths do more maths teaching.
8. The percentage of the age-group getting degree-level qualifications in 1981 was US 22 per cent, Japan 25 per cent, Germany and UK 13 per cent. (Source: *UNESCO Statistical Year Book* 1984; numbers getting level 6 qualification as percentage of average cohort aged 20–24).
9. Manpower Services Commission, *Labour Market Quarterly Report GB*, September 1985.

10. Prais (1981), Table 4; and Prais and Wagner (1983), Tables 1, 2 and 3.
11. Engineering Industry Training Board, *Annual Report*, 1984/5. See also Cantor and Roberts (1983), which shows that manufacturing apprenticeships declined from a stock of 236,000 in 1968 to 100,000 in 1982.
12. This relates to such training provided for one or more days a week, and does not include evenings only. Source: Department of Education and Science, *Statistics of Education*, 1985, Table 19. This includes training by employers.
13. Confederation of British Industry (1984).
14. If there were perfect capital markets and perfect foresight, this would not be true, and workers would finance their own training where this was general (i.e. as useful in one firm as in another). But with imperfect capital markets and uncertainty, it is easy to show that social welfare could be improved by policies which generate more training.
15. 3-digit level minimum list heading.
16. Hughes and McCormick (1982) show how council house tenants are much less likely to migrate than others.
17. Generous migration subsidies could also be used for the long-term unemployed. They cannot be made generally available, as the deadweight cost is too great.

CHAPTER 10 A viable incomes policy

1. See Chapter 3, note 1. This equation is broadly consistent with the more sophisticated results of Wadhwani (1985), using quarterly data.
2. Wadhwani (1985).
3. The evidence is summarized in Layard (1986). The evidence relating to nationalized industries is based on Foster, Henry, and Trinder (1985).
4. The unemployment rates relate to the seven largest OECD countries, which account for 85 per cent of OECD production. They are the standardized rates shown in OECD, *Economic Outlook*, Table R12.
5. Inflation refers to the backward-looking 12-monthly change in the Retail Price Index. The comparison is given in the Department of Employment *Gazette*, Table 6.8, and in OECD *Economic Outlook*, Table R11. Note that inflation in the UK when the Conservatives

came to power in 1979 was only 10.6 per cent. The broad annual inflation picture as shown by the GDP deflator is shown in Figure 11. Note the fact that this rose very little in 1979.

6. Many other options have been advocated. The main ones are discussed in my book *More Jobs Less Inflation*, Chapter 9, where I explain why I consider them infeasible. This book is now out of print but I can supply copies.

7. Brown, W. (1980).

8. This is discussed more fully in my book *More Jobs Less Inflation*. See also Jackman and Layard (1982).

9. This analysis is based on Jackman and Layard (1986a) and Jackman and Layard (1986b). The first assumes perfect competition and the latter imperfect competition. In each case price-setting is not a simple mark-up, so that the counter-inflation tax reduces real wages (as viewed by firms). However it would be misleading to show this implication in Figure 27 without at the same time pointing out that a lower NAIRU would generate higher tax receipts, making possible lower taxes. It would also raise the capital stock in the medium term. So real after-tax wages would be likely to rise rather than fall. For a simple summary of the argument in Jackman and Layard (1986a), see Appendix 4, pp. 88–90 in Blanchard *et al.* (1986).

10. Note the small number of workers in the public sector with real 'industrial muscle'. As a percentage of the total labour force, we have miners 1.1, electricity workers 0.7, gas workers 0.4, water workers 0.2, and dockers 0.6; 3.0 in total.

11. This is only so if inflation is stable. Rising inflation would hurt public sector workers and a decrease in inflation would benefit them.

12. This was a feature of the Treasury's analysis (1985), so often quoted by Nigel Lawson.

13. The Treasury analysis allowed for tax cuts, resulting from a higher tax base. Thus in fact the living standards of workers barely fell when wage pressure was reduced. Given this, it is extraordinary that the Chancellor spent so much time saying that *real* wages had to fall rather than that *nominal* wages had to be lower than they would otherwise have been.

14. It is implausible that profit-sharing *per se* could be an effective alternative to incomes policy as a way of altering the NAIRU. First, it would take a long time to come in. Second, its alleged effects on the NAIRU depend on workers involved in profit-sharing having no

say in employment decisions; this is most unlikely to happen. Third, profit-share formulas have to hold over a long time whatever happens to economic circumstances—again unlikely. For a more optimistic view see Weitzman (1984).

15. Ashenfelter and Layard (1983).
16. Layard, Piachaud, and Stewart (1978).
17. The main criticism of incomes policy in Brittan and Lilley (1977) is that it must necessarily get mixed up with redistribution. But this cannot be inevitable, and was not even the case after 1976.

CHAPTER 11   Aggregate demand and sound finance

1. Minford (1980). See also Sargent and Wallace (1975), and Barro (1977).
2. Lawson (1984).
3. For a full discussion of these models see Davies (1985).
4. Public borrowing does not include borrowing to replace debt which matures, since there should be no problem in borrowing back money which becomes available in this way.
5. This it the fear invoked by Congdon (1985).
6. This is the gross flow of purchases (and sales)—not the change in the stock of bonds outstanding, which is relatively tiny.
7. France and Italy still have them.
8. Suppose the US interest rates are 10 per cent, British interest rates 15 per cent, and the expected fall in the pound 5 per cent. Then if a US citizen invests in pounds for a year and then switches back to dollars, he loses 5 per cent on the exchange rate but gets 15 per cent interest. So he gets 10 per cent in all, which is what he would have got in the US.
9. The latter is the famous Dornbusch 'overshooting' proposition. It is most simply explained as follows. Suppose i is the short-run interest rate and i^* the equivalent world rate, p is current annual inflation and p^* current annual world inflation, and $\dot{e}$ is expected annual depreciation. Then, given no risk premium, expected returns are equalized, so

$$i - i^* = \dot{e},$$

and

$$i - p - (i^* - p^*) = \dot{e} + \dot{p}^* - p.$$

The latter is the expected change in competitiveness, $e + p^* + p$, where p is log prices and p^* is log world prices. We now assume that people expect competitiveness to fall by some proportion γ of its excess over its long run level c. So

$$\dot{e} + p^* - p = \gamma[c - (e+p^*-p)].$$

Thus putting the two relationships together,

$$i - p - (i^* - p^*) = \gamma[c - (e+p^*-p)].$$

If a country is very uncompetitive, people expect its currency to depreciate in real terms and its real interest rate must therefore be high. The opposite also applies. Thus, real interest rates need not be equalized, even when there is no risk premium. Note that differences between actual and expected inflation are not a problem if we confine ourselves to short-run interest rates.

10. There is also no relation between real interest differentials and the trade balance/GDP ratio, which indicates the required capital inflow.

11. The intertemporal budget constraint for foreign borrowing requires that ultimately we run a trade balance sufficient to service our net debt.

12. Suppose imports went up by 5 per cent and the sum of import and export price elasticities were 2. To correct the trade balance would require a 5 per cent increase in competitiveness.

13. The EMS exchange rate is of course a nominal rate. The real exchange rate (or competitiveness) would change if our inflation rates differed from other countries. At present they are in line, but a major divergence could always be offset by a renegotiation of the EMS rate.

CHAPTER 12 **Alternative policies**

1. David Grubb at the L.S.E. Centre for Labour Economics has performed the following regressions (average coefficients and t-statistics for 19 OECD countries 1952–82):

$$\dot{w} = \text{constant} + 0.70\dot{p}_{-1} + 0.30\dot{w}_{-1} - 0.33(w-p)_{-1}$$
$$\qquad\qquad\qquad (3.0) \qquad\qquad (1.5)$$

$$- 1.9l + 2.0n - 0.2h + 0.2t,$$
$$(1.6) \quad (2.3) \quad (0.2) \quad (0.3)$$

where w = log hourly earnings in manufacturing, p = log prices (consumption deflator), l = log labour force, n = log employment, h = log average weekly hours per worker in manufacturing, and t = time. This shows that hours per worker play no role. In other work (Grubb, 1986) he has shown that output is not as good at explaining inflation as unemployment is (the t-statistic is only 25 per cent of the t-statistic on unemployment).

Two simple models illustrate why hours might have no effect. In the first model unions set real hourly wages. Each ith union faces a demand curve for its labour (N_i). Subject to that, it maximizes the expected income of its members (who number M_i). Expected income $E(Y)$ is

$$E(Y) = N_i H W_i + (M_i - N_i) H W (1 - U),$$

where W_i is the union's real wage, W is the economy-wide real wage, H is the hours per worker (exogenous), and U is the national unemployment rate. Thus

$$E(Y) = N_i H [W_i - W(1 - U)] + \text{constant}.$$

If the demand curve for labour is $N_i H = f(W_i)$, then hours do not appear in the union's maximand. More generally, the first-order condition for wages is

$$[W_i - W(1 - U)] \frac{\partial N_i}{\partial W_i} + N_i = 0.$$

For general equilibrium we set $W_i = W$, so that

$$U = \frac{1}{\eta},$$

where η is the elasticity of demand for labour in the demand curve which the union faces. There is no obvious reason why this should depend on H. Hence U is independent of H.

In the second model, imperfectly competitive firms set real hourly wages. They are worried about quitting because the net output per worker is $H\gamma(1 - \theta Q)$ where Q, the quit rate, depends on expected income in the firm relative to outside. Thus the profit of the ith firm is

$$\Pi_I = N_i H \left[\gamma - \gamma \theta Q \left(\frac{W_i}{W(1-U)} \right) - W_i \right].$$

This is maximized subject to the firm's demand curve. The optimum price requires that marginal revenue per unit of output equal marginal cost. So

$$P_i \left(1 - \frac{1}{\eta'} \right) = \frac{W_i}{\gamma[1 - \theta Q(.)]},$$

where P_i is the firm's relative price and η' the price elasticity of demand for its product. This condition is independent of H. Similarly the condition for the optimal wage is independent of H. Thus equilibrium U is independent of H. It is not difficult to produce plausible variants where $\partial U/\partial H < 0$, and more difficult to produce variants where $\partial U/\partial H > 0$ (see, for example, Johnson and Layard 1986).

2. No undertakings to the contrary have emerged from the trade union movement as part of its campaign for a shorter working week.

3. For a more sympathetic analysis, see Dreze (1986).

4. OECD, *Employment Outlook*, September 1985, p. 107.

5. OECD, *Labour Force Statistics*.

6. A man aged 64 (or woman aged 59) can retire a year early and be paid £65.50 (if married) or £52 (if single), if his/her employer agrees to replace him/her by an unemployed person. There is also a part-time Job Release Scheme open to men aged 62–64 and women aged 59 by which the worker gets roughly half the standard allowance for going part time, provided his/her employer recruits an unemployed person as a result of the arrangement. The schemes now have 50,000 people on them.

7. He will actually get the Supplementary Benefit level + £4 (disregard) minus Earnings.

List of Figures and Tables

FIGURES

TABLES

Notes to Figures and Tables

Throughout this book the unemployment rate is calculated as the number unemployed relative to the labour force (*excluding* the self-employed), except where otherwise stated.

Three main definitions of unemployment are used; the definition used is indicated where it is not obvious.

(i) *'Pre-1982' official definition*: Based on unemployed registrants at employment exchanges.

(ii) *'Post-1982' official definition*: Based on unemployed claimants of benefits or National Insurance credits (affecting their future pension rights). In October 1982, this reduced measured unemployment by about 50,000 males and 100,000 females, who were not claimants. Subsequently, in 1983, men over 60 were no longer required to sign on at benefit offices in order to obtain National Insurance credits, and this reduced measured male unemployment by around a further 200,000. (See Unemployment Unit, Bulletin no. 11, January 1984.)

(iii) *Survey definition*: People saying they are out of work and seeking work, in reply to survey questionnaires (e.g. OPCS, *General Household Survey*). This is US practice. The OECD standardized rates aim in this direction, but are not for Britain based on actual survey data.

FIGURES

Figure 1

This aims to measure unemployment on the 'pre-1982' definition.

(i) Up to 1920 the data are based on trade union records and come from Feinstein (1972), Table 57.

(ii) From 1921–38 the data are based on counts of the insured unemployed, adjusted on the basis of the 1931 Census to include workers not covered by National Insurance. Our figures come from Feinstein, Table 58.

(iii) From 1939–82 the data are the official figures for unemployed registered at employment exchanges (Department of Employment, *Gazette*.) Employees in employment after 1959 are taken from CSO, *Economic Trends Annual Supplement*, 1985; the figures for before 1959 are the total in civil employment (Feinstein, Table 57) less estimated self-employed.

(iv) Since 1982 unemployment figures are estimated on the pre-1982 basis by the Unemployment Unit, Bulletin no. 11, January 1984, and subsequent Statistical Supplements.

Figure 2

Public sector debt measures the total face value of the public debt outstanding at 31 March, less holdings of public debt by government bodies and public corporations. This is expressed as a percentage of Gross Domestic Product at current market prices in the year ending 31 March. From 1968, the figures are given in *Financial Statistics*, February 1979, Table C, and February 1986, Table S1. Before 1968, the source for the debt statistics is the CSO, *Annual Abstract of Statistics*, 1970, Table 327, and for Gross Domestic Product, CSO, *Economic Trends Annual Supplement*, 1984, p. 8.

Figure 3

Unemployed as a percentage of the labour force including self-employed, taken from OECD, *Economic Outlook*, June 1985, Table R12, and previous issues. Before 1966 rates are based on national definitions and are corrected to bring them into line with the OECD standardized measure (OECD, *Labour Force Statistics*, various issues). Figures for 1985 and 1986 are provisional—see OECD, *Economic Outlook*, June 1985, Table 13, p. 28 (the December issue forecasts the same changes).

Figure 4

Department of Employment, *Gazette*, Table 2.8, various issues. Annual averages. Pre-1982 definition. At the time of the changes in the measurement of unemployment, the Department of Employment estimated the numbers affected in the various duration categories and these numbers are added back in for subsequent dates. The resulting male unemployment total is in line with similar estimates made by the Unemployment Unit.

Figure 5

OECD, *Employment Outlook*, September 1985, Table H, p. 126. Unemployment is measured on national definitions.

Figure 6

Department of Employment, *Gazette*, November 1985, p. S6.

Figure 7

Department of Employment (data privately supplied). Unemployment is measured on the post-1982 definition.

Figure 8

Department of Employment, *Gazette*, July 1982, Table 2.9.

Figure 9

Employment and labour force both include self-employed. Employment data is taken from OECD, *Labour Force Statistics* (various issues). Labour force is defined as total employment divided by 1 − OECD standardized unemployment rate (see sources to Figure 3).

Figure 11

See note 1, Chapter 3. Unemployment is measured on OECD standardized definitions (see sources to Figure 3); the GDP deflator at factor cost is taken from the CSO, *United Kingdom National Accounts*, 1985 and earlier editions, Table 1.16.

Figure 14a

This is an index if $v \log P_m/P$ where v is the share of imports in GDP, and P_m/P is import prices relative to the GDP deflator. For details of calculations and data, see Layard and Nickell (1986), Data Appendix.

Figure 14b

Panels (a) and (b) show, respectively, t_1 and t_2 as measured by Layard and Nickell (1986). The value of t_1 is employers' National Insurance plus firm's contributions to private pension schemes, all expressed as a proportion of the wage and salary bill in that year. (Source: CSO,

United Kingdom National Accounts). Panel (c) is the Factor Cost Adjustment less Selective Employment Tax (1966–73) and National Insurance Surcharge (1977–84) as a proportion of GDP at Factor Cost. (CSO, *United Kingdom National Accounts*, Table 1.2 and Table 7.2.) These two taxes are counted as expenditure taxes for national accounts purposes, but are already included in the measurement of t_1 (panel a).

Figure 15

Jackman, Layard, and Pissarides (1984), Figure 2, updated to 1985. This figure uses the pre-1982 definition of unemployment, and recent figures are corrected to be consistent with this (see sources to Figure 4).

Vacancy data are based on vacancies registered with employment exchanges corrected for the share of the employment exchanges in total vacancies (proxied by the share in all job fillings). Recent data for vacancies are given in Department of Employment, *Gazette*, Table 3.1. These must be corrected to obtain the true picture and the correction factor for 1983–5 assumes only 32.6 per cent of vacancies are reported (See Jackman, Layard, and Pissarides (1985) for details.)

Figure 16

The replacement ratio is the weighted average of ratios for the different family types considered in Table 4, using the weights shown in column (6) of that table. Each family is assumed to have only one earner, whose potential earnings are measured by average male manual earnings. Up to 1969 this is measured by the October earnings survey. From 1970, the Department of Employment *New Earnings Survey* is used to give an equivalent October figure. This figure is then used as average earnings for the tax year commencing the previous April. The relevant tax thresholds, tax rates, and child support (source: CSO, *Annual Abstract of Statistics* and *Inland Revenue Statistics*, 1980) are then applied to calculate a net earnings figure for that tax year.

Supplementary Benefit for the family type from 1950 is published in Department of Health and Social Security, *Social Security Statistics*, 1985. The average weekly benefit for the tax year can thus be calculated. As the Supplementary Benefit scale rate is not intended to cover housing costs, the denominator of the ratio is net earnings multiplied by 1 − housing expenditure as a proportion of total household expenditure. (Source: *Family Expenditure Survey*, from 1963; CSO, *United Kingdom National Accounts* previously.)

Figure 18

Panels (a) and (b): Department of Employment, *British Labour Statistics Historical Abstract*, and Department of Employment, *Gazette*. Panel (c) is calculated from cross-section regressions for the years 1953–83. The method is described in Layard, Metcalf, and Nickell, *British Journal of Industrial Relations*, 1978. This is then standardized around an estimate of the mark-up for 1978 of 8 per cent (Stewart 1983).

Figure 19

Non-oil GDP is calculated by the CSO. It was published in the *Economic Trends Annual Supplement* until the 1982 edition. More recent figures are available upon request.

Figure 20

CSO, *Economic Trends*, p. 46. The figure for 1985 relates to the first two quarters only.

Figures 21, 22 and 23

Up to 1965: Feinstein (1972), Table 57 (working population and employment) and Table 6 (output). From 1965: CSO, *Economic Trends Annual Supplement*, 1985, and CSO, *Economic Trends*. Both the working population and employment are defined to include the armed forces and the self-employed. The measurement of output excludes the impact of North Sea oil (see sources to Figure 20).

Figure 24

Confederation of British Industry, *Industrial Trends Survey*. The figures shown in the graph are annual averages of responses to surveys in January, April, July, and October.

Figure 28

Chart A, 7, OECD, *Economic Outlook*, June 1985. Breaks represent missing data or changed definitions.

Figure 29

For the UK public debt/GDP ratio, see sources to Figure 2. The real interest rate differential is the difference between the UK real interest rate and that for the six other largest OECD countries. The UK rate is the Treasury Bill rate less the rate of change of the GDP deflator at market prices (CSO, *Economic Trends*). The OECD rate is a weighted average of a three month interest rate for each country (OECD, *Main Economic Indicators*), less the rate of change of the OECD GDP at market prices deflator (OECD, *National Accounts*, 1960–83, vol. I, part iii).

Figure 30

The ratio of UK public debt to 'world' public debt is measured in the following way:

$$\frac{\text{UK Debt}}{\text{'World' Debt}} = \left(\frac{\text{UK debt}}{\text{UK GDP}} \middle/ \frac{\text{OECD debt}}{\text{OECD GDP}}\right) \frac{\text{UK GDP}}{\text{OECD GDP}}.$$

The debt/GDP ratios relate to *net* debt, and are given in Muller and Price (1984), Table A3.11. The ratio of UK GDP to OECD GDP is calculated from OECD, *National Accounts*, 1960–83, vol I, part iii. The real interest rate is calculated as in Figure 29.

TABLES

Table 1

OECD, *Employment Outlook*, September 1985, Table G, p. 126. All figures are unemployed divided by total labour force (including self-employed). The unemployment figures are as measured by national definitions, but these differ in their implications much less in the case of men than of women.

Table 2

OPCS, *Labour Force Survey*, 1981, Table 4.19. The figures relate to the stock of unemployed, as measured by the survey, and exclude some 6.5 per cent who did not reply or give their reasons.

Table 3

Department of Employment, *Gazette*, July 1977, p. 719 and Table 2.15, April 1982 and August 1985. Figures for 1976 and 1980 relate to Great Britain; 1985 also includes Northern Ireland. Unemployment is measured according to current definitions.

Table 4

Current rates of benefit are taken from Smith and Rowland (1986) and Cohen and Lakhani (1986). All figures relate to householders. Earnings are based on the rate for a male manual worker on average earnings, using data from the Department of Employment, *New Earnings Survey* (1985) and assuming an annual rate of wage inflation of 8 per cent. Married couples without children are assumed to earn the average wage, couples with children 5 per cent above, and single householders 20 per cent below. These assumptions are based on the OPCS *General Household Survey*, 1982. Each family is assumed to live in local authority rented accommodation appropriate to the family type and pay average rent and rates for that family type. Estimates of housing costs by family type are given in Department of Health and Social Security *Tax/Benefit Model Tables*. The proportions of the male unemployed by family type are taken from the OPCS *General Household Survey* 1983, Table 7.24.

Table 5

J. Mallender and S. Ramsden, 'Incomes in and out of work 1978–1982: results using the DHSS Cohort Simulation Model'. Government Economic Service Working Paper No. 69, 1984.

Table 6

Data suplied by the Department of Health and Social Security. They also include a small number of people who failed to carry out reasonable recommendations given in writing by their job centre or employment office to help them find suitable employment.

Table 7

Columns (1) to (3), Jackman and Roper (1985), Table 1, Index I_1. Columns (4) and (5) are from Jackman, Layard, and Pissarides (1984), Table 5. In the first column there is a break: from 1973 onwards the data relate to 18 occupations, before 1973 to 24.

Table 8

Columns (1) to (3) are calculated from the CSO *United Kingdom National Accounts* 1985 and previous editions. Column (2) excludes payments to the unemployed (*Annual Abstract of Statistics*, Table 3.5, making some allowance for the switch to Housing Benefit in 1982/3). It also includes 'real' interest payments, which are estimated by multiplying government debt in market hands by a three year moving average of the real interest rate in column (4). Potential GDP is calculated by taking 1977 as a base, and assuming an annual real growth rate of $2\frac{1}{2}$ per cent. (This includes the effect of North Sea oil). Column (4) is the Treasury Bill 3-month rate less the current rate of change in the Retail Price Index (*Economic Trends* and CSO, *Economic Trends Annual Supplement*, 1986). For column (5), see sources to Figure 20.

Table 9

Department of Employment, *Gazette*, Table 1.2. Figures exclude Northern Ireland.

Table 11

Department of Employment, *Gazette*, Table 2.4 (by region) and Table 2.15 (by age). The latest figures by industry are for April 1982 (Department of Employment, *Gazette*, July 1982, Table 2.8) and these have been adjusted to correspond to the current unemployment total. Rates by skill are from the OPCS *General Household Survey*, 1983, Table 2.8. Again these have been adjusted to be on a comparable basis with the other figures. All unemployment rates correspond to the current (post-1982) definition of the unemployed.

Table 13

Prais (1981). For data on US and Japan, see also Institute of Manpower Studies (1984), especially Table 6.6.

Table 14

Data supplied by the Manpower Services Commission.

References

Ashenfelter, O. and Layard, P. R. G. (1983), 'Incomes Policy and Wage Differentials', *Economica*, May.

Atkinson, A. B. and Micklewright, J. (1982), 'Work Expenses and Replacement Ratio Calculations', Unemployment Project Working Note 13.

Barro, R. J. (1977), 'Unanticipated Money Growth and Unemployment in the United States', *American Economic Review* 67, pp. 101–15.

Beveridge, W. (1942), *Social Insurance and Allied Services*, Cmd. 6404, HMSO.

Blanchard, O., Dornbusch, R., Dreze, J., Giersch, H., Layard, P. R. G., and Monti, M. (1985), 'Employment Growth in Europe: A Two-Handed Approach', 1985 Report of the CEPS Macroeconomic Policy Group, Centre for Economic Policy Studies, Brussels.

Blanchard, O., Dornbusch, R., and Layard, P. R. G. (1986), *Restoring Europe's Prosperity*, Centre for European Policy Studies, Brussels.

Blanchard, O. and Summers, L. (1986), 'Hysteresis and the European Unemployment Problem', Massachusetts Institute of Technology, mimeo, March.

Bosworth, D. L. and Dawkins, P. J. (1980), 'Shiftworking and Unsocial Hours', *Industrial Relations Journal*, 11, pp. 32–40.

Brittan, S. and Lilley, P. (1977), *The Delusion of Incomes Policy*, London.

Brown, W. (1980), 'The Structure of Pay Bargaining in Britain', in Blackaby, F. (ed.), *The Future of Pay Bargaining*, NIESR, London: Heinemann.

Budd, A., Levine, P., and Smith, P. (1985), 'Unemployment, Vacancies and the Long-Term Unemployed', London Business School, Centre for Economic Forecasting, Discussion Paper no. 154.

Buiter, W. H. and Miller, M. (1983), 'The Macroeconomic Consequences of a Change in Regime', *Brookings Papers in Economic Activity*.

Cantor, L. M. and Roberts, I. F. (1983), *Further Education Today*, London.

Central Statistical Office, *Annual Abstract of Statistics*, annual.

Central Statistical Office, *Economic Trends*, monthly.

Central Statistical Office, *Economic Trends Annual Supplement*, annual.

Central Statistical Office, *United Kingdom National Accounts*, annual.

Cohen, R., and Lakhani, B. (1986), *National Welfare Benefits Handbook*, 15th ed., Child Poverty Action Group.

Confederation of British Industry (1984), *Attitudes towards Unemployment*, Confederation of British Industry Social Affairs Directorate, November.

Confederation of British Industry (1985), *Cutting Unemployment Now: The Opportunity for the 1986 Budget*, November.

Confederation of British Industry (1986), 'Growth and Jobs', *Confederation of British Industry News*, January.

Confederation of British Industry, *Industrial Trends Survey*, quarterly.

Congdon, T. (1985), *The Debt Trap*, Messel Brothers, London.

Daniel, W. and Stigloe, E. (1978), *The Impact of Employment Protection Laws*, Policy Studies Institute, London.

Davies, G. (1985), *Governments Can Affect Employment*, Employment Institute, London.

Davies, G. and Metcalf, D. H. (1985), 'Generating Jobs', *The Economics Analyst*, Simon and Coates, April.

Department of Employment, *Gazette*, monthly.

Department of Employment, *Family Expenditure Survey*, annual.

Department of Employment, *New Earnings Survey*, annual.

Department of Employment and Department of Health and Social Security (1981), *Payments of Benefits to Unemployed People*, March.

Department of Health and Social Security, *Social Security Statistics*, annual.

Department of Health and Social Security, *Unemployment Benefit Statistics*, annual.

Dilnot, A. W., Kay, J. A., and Morris, C. N. (1984), *The Reform of Social Security*, Oxford.

Dilnot, A. W. and Morris, C. N. (1984), 'Private Costs and Benefits of Unemployment: Measuring Replacement Rates', in C. A. Greenhalgh, P. R. G. Layard and A. J. Oswald (eds), *The Causes of Unemployment*, Oxford.

Dreze, J. (1985), *Work Sharing: Why? How? How Not*, Commission of the European Communities, Directorate-General for Economic and Financial Affairs.

Feinstein, C. H. (1972), *National Income and Expenditure in the United Kingdom, 1855–1965*, Cambridge.

Forsyth, P. and Kay, J. A. (1980), 'The Economic Implications of North Sea Oil Revenues', *Fiscal Studies*, July.

Foster, N., Henry, S. G. B. and Trinder, C. (1985), 'Public and private sector pay, some further results', NIESR, mimeo.

Freeman, R. B. and Wise, D. A. (1978). *The Youth Labour Market Problem, Its Nature, Causes and Consequences*, Harvard.

Grubb, D., Jackman, R. A. and Layard, P. R. G. (1982), 'Causes of Current Stagflation', *Review of Economic Studies*, October.

HM Treasury (1985), *The Relationship Between Employment and Wages*, London.

House of Commons (1986), *Special Employment Measures and the Long-Term Unemployed*, First Report from the Employment Committee, Session 1985/6.

Hughes, G. and McCormick, B. (1981), 'Do Council Housing Policies Reduce Migration Between Regions?', *Economic Journal*, December.

Institute of Manpower Studies (1984), *Competence and Competition*, NEDO.

Jackman, R. A. and Layard, P. R. G. (1982), 'An Inflation Tax', *Fiscal Studies*, March.

Jackman, R. A. and Layard, P. R. G. (1986a), 'The Economic Effects of Tax-Based Incomes Policy' and 'Is TIP Administratively Feasible', chapters 6 and 9 of D. C. Colander (ed.) *Incentive-Based Incomes Policies*, Ballinger, Cambridge, Mass.

Jackman, R. A. and Layard, P. R. G. (1986b), 'A Wage-Tax, Worker-Subsidy Policy for Reducing the "Natural" Rate of Unemployment', in W. Beckerman (ed.), *Wage Rigidity and Unemployment*, Duckworth.

Jackman, R. A., Layard, P. R. G. and Metcalf, D. H. (1985), 'How to Reduce Unemployment Without Increasing Inflation', paper presented to the Conference on Unemployment and Selective Policy Intervention by the Government in the UK Labour Market, Policy Studies Institute.

Jackman, R. A., Layard, P. R. G. and Pissarides, C. (1985), 'On Vacancies', London School of Economics, Centre for Labour Economics, Discussion Paper no. 165 (revised).

Jackman, R. A. and Roper, S. N. (1985), 'Structural Unemployment', London School of Economics, Centre for Labour Economics, Discussion Paper no. 233.

Johnson, G. E. and Layard, P. R. G. (1986), 'The Natural Rate of Unemployment and Labour Market Policy', in O. Ashenfelter and P. R. G. Layard (eds.), *Handbook of Labor Economics,* North Holland,

Amsterdam.

Lawson, N. (1984), 'The British Experiment' Fifth Mais Lecture, City University Business School, London, June.

Layard, P. R. G. (1982), *More Jobs, Less Inflation*, Grant McIntyre, London.

Layard, P. R. G. (1986), 'Public Sector Pay: The British Perspective', London School of Economics, Centre for Labour Economics, Discussion Paper no. 229.

Layard, P. R. G., Basevi, G., Blanchard, O., Buiter, W. H. and Dornbusch, R. (1984), 'Europe: The Case for Unsustainable Growth', Centre for European Policy Studies, paper no. 8/9.

Layard, P. R. G., Metcalf, D. and O'Brien, R. (1986), 'A New Deal for the Long-Term Unemployed', in P. E. Hart (ed.), *Unemployment and Labour Market Policies*, Gower, London.

Layard, P. R. G. and Nickell, S. J. (1980), 'The Case for Subsidising Extra Jobs', *Economic Journal*, March.

Layard, P. R. G. and Nickell, S. J. (1986), 'Unemployment in Britain', *Economica*, supplement.

Layard, P. R. G., Piachaud, D. and Stewart, M. (1978), *The Causes of Poverty*, Royal Commission on the Distribution of Income and Wealth, Background Paper no. 5, HMSO.

Metcalf, D., Nickell, S. J. and Floros, N. (1982), 'Still Searching for an Explanation of Unemployment in Inter-War Britain', *Journal of Political Economy*, April.

Micklewright, J. (1983), 'Male Unemployment and the Family Expenditure Survey, 1972–80', Social Science Research Council Programme: Taxation, Incentives, and the Distribution of Income, Working Paper no. 47.

Minford, P. (1980), 'A Rational Expectations Model of the United Kingdom Under Fixed and Floating Exchange Rates', in K. Brunner and A. H. Meltzer (eds.), *The State of Macroeconomics*, Carnegie–Rochester Conference Series on Public Policy, no. 12, pp. 293–355.

Minford, P. (1985), *Unemployment, Cause and Cure*, 2nd edition, Blackwell Oxford.

Moylan, S., Millar, J. and Davies, R. (1984), *For Richer for Poorer? DHSS Cohort Study of Unemployed Men*, Department of Health and Social Security, Social Research Branch, Research Report no. 11.

Muller, P. and Price, R. W. R. (1984), 'Structural Budget Deficits and Fiscal Stance', Organization for Economic Co-operation and Development, Economics and Statistics Department, Working Paper no. 15.

Narendranathan, W., Nickell, S. J. and Stern, J. (1985), 'Unemployment Benefits Revisited', *Economic Journal*, June.

National Economic Development Office (1985), *Investment in the Public Sector-Built Infrastructure*.

National Labour Market Board, Unemployment Insurance Division, Sweden (1984), *Cash Unemployment Assistance*.

Nissim, J. (1984), 'The Price Responsiveness of the Demand for Labour by Skill: British Mechanical Engineering, 1963–78', *Economic Journal*, December.

Office of Population, Census and Surveys, *General Household Survey*, annual.

Office of Population, Census and Surveys, *Labour Force Survey*, alternate years until 1983, thereafter annual.

Organization for Economic Co-operation and Development (1982), *The Challenge of Unemployment*, Paris.

Organization for Economic Co-operation and Development *Economic Outlook*, bi-annual.

Organization for Economic Co-operation and Development *Employment Outlook*, annual.

Organization for Economic Co-operation and Development *Labour Force Statistics*.

Organization for Economic Co-operation and Development *Main Economic Indicators*.

Organization for Economic Co-operation and Development, *National Accounts*.

Pahl, R. E. (1984), *Divisions of Labour*, Blackwell, Oxford.

Prais, S. J. and Wagner, K. (1983), 'Some Practical Aspects of Human Capital Investment: Training Standards in Five Occupations in Britain and Germany', *National Institute Economic Review*, August.

Prais, S. J. and Wagner, K. (1983), 'Some Practical Aspects of Human Capital Investment: Training Standards in Five Occupations in Britain and Germany', *National Institute Economic Review*, August.

Prais, S. J. and Wagner, K. (1985), 'Schooling Standards in England and Germany: Some Summary Comparisons Bearing on Economic Performance', *National Institute Economic Review*, May.

Sargent, T. J. and Wallace, N. (1975), 'Rational Expectations, the Optimal Monetary Instrument and the Optimal Money Supply Rule', *Journal of Political Economy*, 83, p. 241.

Smith, R. and Rowland, M. (1986), *Rights Guide to Non-Means Tested Social Security Benefits*, 8th edn., Child Poverty Action Group.

Stewart, M. (1983), 'Relative Earnings and Individual Union Membership in the UK', *Economica*, May.

Thatcher, A. R. (1968), 'The Distribution of Earnings of Employees in Great Britain', *Journal of the Royal Statistical Society*, series A, no. 131, pp. 131–80.

Treasury and Civil Service Committee (1983), *The Structure of Personal Income Taxation and Income Support: Third Special Report*.

Unemployment Unit, *Bulletin*, Unemployment Unit, 9 Poland Street, London W1.

Wadhwani, S. (1985), 'Wage Inflation in the UK', *Economica*, May.

Weitzman, M. (1984), *The Share Economy*, Harvard.

Wells, W. (1983), 'The Relative Pay and Employment of Young People', Department of Employment Research Paper no. 42, October.

Wilson, Lord (1980), Committee to Review the Functioning of Financial Institutions, Cmnd. 7937, Research Reports 1 and 3.

Index

This index is intended to serve also as a glossary. References which define and explain terms are shown in **bold** type.

Only economic variables.

A was drastic = unemployment / inflation